AF579315

SOME UNSEEN POWER

Some Unseen Power

Diary of a Ghost-Hunter

by

PHILIP PAUL

Foreword by
Professor Keith Simpson
CBE MA MD LLD FRCP FRCPath DMJ

ROBERT HALE · LONDON

First published in Great Britain 1985

ISBN 0 7090 2384 7

Robert Hale Limited
Clerkenwell House
Clerkenwell Green
London EC1R 0HT

British Library Cataloguing in Publication Data

Paul, Philip
Some unseen power: diary of a ghost hunter
1. Ghosts
1. Title
133.1′092′4 BF1461

ISBN 0-7090-2384-7

Photoset in North Wales by
Derek Doyle & Associates, Mold, Clwyd
Printed in Great Britain by
St. Edmundsbury Press, Bury St. Edmunds, Suffolk
Bound by Woolnough Bookbinding, Northants

Contents

To Joan
without whose encouragement these words
would not have been written
and for
those who seek in this world and those
who have discovered, beyond

Illustrations

Between pages 80 and 81

The awful shadow of some unseen Power
Floats though unseen among us, visiting
This various world with as inconstant wing
As summer winds that creep from flower to flower.

Percy Bysshe Shelley 1792–1822

Hymn to Intellectual Beauty

Foreword

by

Professor Keith Simpson

CBE MA MD LLD FRCP FRCPath DMJ

University Professor of Forensic Medicine, London

Home Office Pathologist

At the time, in 1953, when Gilbert Harding made one of his notorious jibes – "You believe in ghosts – you must be barmy!" in the BBC's *What's My Line?* – at the author of this book, I was an agnostic materialist, a young Home Office pathologist demanding firm physical proof of life or death: a stroke or a strangling, a coronary or cancer. Haunted houses like the famous Borley Rectory, extrasensory phenomena, ghosts, the pranks of poltergeists, and even the serious studies of reputably clear-thinking men like Sir Oliver Lodge, Sir Arthur Conan Doyle or Sir William Crookes, left me unbelieving. Gilbert Harding, then living as I did at 1 Weymouth Street, had little trouble in fortifying my disbelief. "Quite right, dear sir," he bellowed. "Absolute nonsense!"

Does anything survive death? Is a spirit detectable by any physical means? What, I used to ask myself, would an Old Bailey jury think of a pathologist who attributed a battered head to offended spirits? No, I felt then, quite firmly: I cannot indulge in such fantasy.

Yet this remarkable book by Philip Paul persuades me to think seriously about such phenomena. Here is a sane thinking man, an experienced journalist and critical assessor, not easily given to a hollow cause, setting out authenticated happenings that demand serious attention. These pages are the diary of a man who has, by his sober approaches, achieved a solid repute in his studies.

Philip Paul's highly rational attitudes compel attention, and when, as throughout this fascinating book, his pen runs so smoothly, it is indeed a pleasure to read – and difficult to put down. His experiences never sound bogus for they are in sepia, not the lurid colours of a man carried away by conviction. Paul is alert for fraud and deception, looking as every journalist might for a scandal and exposure.

Somehow, against my scientific training, I am induced to accept the author's persuasion: he is such a reliable sounding recorder of fact, not given to exaggerate or to be carried away by *naïveté.* He writes so readably and his many *coups d'oeuil* of the long stream of distinguished friends and acquaintances he has had make this volume a diary that is original and highly readable.

Keith Simpson
London, 1985

Acknowledgements

I am indebted to many people who have helped, in a variety of ways, towards production of this book. It is not possible to name everyone, but I thank them all. Particular gratitude is expressed to the following, for special assistance. The late Maurice Barbanell, former editor of *Psychic News, Two Worlds* and *Psychic World* for permission to quote extracts from those journals. Tony Ortzen, now editor of *Psychic News* and *Two Worlds*, for generous aid with bibliographical and other research. Bernsen's International Press Service Ltd, for permission to reproduce the photograph showing me in conversation with James Laver and Dr Gerald Gardner. Leonard Sewell, for his extensive help with my work at Borley and for the excellent photographic record he provided of my two years of excavations there. G. Alan Walker, for the provision of regular bulletins and other material regarding the Runcorn poltergeist. Cheshire County Newspapers, for permission to quote extracts from the *Runcorn Guardian* concerning the Runcorn poltergeist and to reproduce the photograph of the 'poltergeist boy' in his wrecked bedroom. *Runcorn Weekly News*, for permission to quote extracts from that newspaper's coverage of the Runcorn poltergeist outbreak. Clifford and Joan Davies, for their generous hospitality and help in investigating the Runcorn poltergeist. BBC Hulton Picture Library, for permission to reproduce the photograph showing me with Gilbert Harding at *Picture Post*'s 1953 Christmas party. The *Daily Express*, for permission to reproduce the 'Artie' cartoon 'Do you really believe in Gilbert Harding?' Associated Newspapers Group plc, for permission to reproduce the *Daily Sketch* photograph of Ena Twigg psychometrizing the 'evil' painting. Gordon Hibbs, for his assistance in unravelling the mystery of the 'dead miner' photograph and for other help and hospitality. My friends Bernard and Jeanette Rosen, formerly of New York and now of California, for much kindness, hospitality and many hundreds of miles of transportation during sundry investigatory excursions in the USA. E.P. Dutton, of New York, for permission to use an extract from *Spindrift*, by Jan Bryant Bartell. Gordon Moore, village clerk of Amityville, New York, for information about events before, during and following the Amityville disturbance. Detective Sergeant Patrick Cammaroto, of Amityville Police Department, for his co-operation in establishing facts about the Amityville disturbance. Dr Roger Curtiss, of the British Animal Health Trust, for information about the visual faculties of nocturnally-active animals. New York journalist Geoffrey Blyth, for information in respect of events connected with the Amityville disturbance. My friends Anna Ford, Ronald Bedford, Dr Brian Inglis and Professor Keith Simpson, for kind help. My agent, Miss Amanda Little, of Watson, Little Ltd. for expert guidance and encouragement. Miss Hazel Maxted, for meticulous typing and re-typing of the work, entailing the burning of much 'midnight oil'.

Philip Paul

Introduction

This modest work does not seek to propagate any specific belief, concept or theory. The words that follow are not aimed at presenting, or destroying, any argument, philosophy or contention.

This is the simple chronicle of an inquiring journalist who has devoted time to the study of manifestations relating to two of mankind's most perplexing puzzles – do paranormalities occur and does the human personality survive the death of the body? It deals primarily with factual events and only secondarily with supposition and conjecture.

Of one supremely important factor the reader may be assured. Insofar as may be attained by the best endeavours within the limits of human fallibility, every word is true.

Philip Paul
Reform Club
London
1985

1. How It Began

My mother's screams woke me in the darkness. Shocked into consciousness, I rushed from my bedroom. From the bathroom at the opposite end of the landing came my brother, Ralph. He was carrying a slim white body whose dangling limbs dripped water. It was my sister, Doris. Seven years my senior, she was seven years younger than my brother. Making his career in the Royal Air Force, Ralph was not long home from India, where he had been in the midst of an earthquake which killed thousands and devastated the town of Quetta, on the North West Frontier.

Gently, he lowered her to the floor. Her eyes were closed but her mouth was slightly open, just revealing her teeth. Her blonde hair, darkened by immersion, trickled water onto the carpet. Quickly, he told me how to help apply artificial respiration. Kneeling by her head and grasping her wrists, I pumped her arms rhythmically up and down in time with his pressures on her ribs. I shall always remember the feeling of moving those arms. It was like lifting the sleeves of an empty garment.

We worked in silence for what seemed an age. In fact it was probably between a quarter and half an hour. My heart thumping, I prayed silently for her return to us. A little water came from her mouth but her eyes stayed closed. I began to realize that the familiar being I had known – and now knew I loved – so well had slipped beyond the reach of hands or entreaties. At last Ralph stood up. 'You can stop,' he said. 'She's dead.'

So, as a boy that bleak Saturday night in February 1938, in my father's house in Alexandra Park, North London, I first saw death and the naked human female and first experienced the anguish called bereavement.

With hindsight, after a war that annihilated millions, the loss of a young sister cannot appear as an exceptional event. But her end came at a time when death in youth was not commonplace as the price of international hostility. The gruesome slaughter of 1914-18 was receding from public memory; the more technological bloodbath of 1939-45 had yet to come.

My father, a railway stationmaster, arrived home from late duty to find the house occupied by doctors, ambulance men and police. My mother had been sedated and was being comforted by neighbours. It was another horror to see him, normally an undemonstrative individual, crumble into sobs, running his fingers through the white hair on his bowed head. It was a wound from which he never recovered, the worst of several misfortunes which had befallen us since moving into the house four years earlier. From that day he became more subdued and withdrawn, until his death, after a long and agonizing struggle against cancer, eleven years later.

A *post-mortem* revealed that Doris had died of haemorrhage from a duodenal ulcer. The abrupt ending of a closely related life that I had come to take entirely for granted brought with it a crushing realization of human frailty and the transience of happiness.

There followed the torment of irremediable regrets. Why hadn't I treated her more kindly, shown her greater generosity and understanding? I sensed my parents thinking similarly. My mother, a temperamental Norfolkwoman, had by no means overwhelmed us with overt maternal affection. Now she pleaded with our aloof and patently embarrassed Church of England pastor for some assurance of her daughter's survival. My father, who had so often complained when Doris tuned the radio to dance music from Luxembourg, looked sadly at the dials her fingers would move no more. Her much-criticized collection of cosmetics – 'Do you have to put that muck on your face?' – became precious mementoes. Even a cigarette burn she had caused on a brand-new mahogany overmantel took on the role of a cherished reminder.

An attractive young woman who had never wanted for male admirers, she had announced a wish to get into show business. That ambition had been squashed by our parents, who feared for her moral welfare in such an occupation. So she had gone into the fashion world, working for the well-known designer Captain Molyneux and later as a model/sales assistant in a Knightsbridge gown shop.

Shortly before her death, she had been engaged to a good-looking but deceitful young man from Nottingham. His unfeeling ending of the attachment coincided with the loss of her job. Desolate, she had spent many hours sitting at home, occasionally complaining of internal pain. Several times my mother suggested consulting the family doctor. Doris always refused. She was modest to a point that seems unbelievable in this present permissive age; she did not want to be examined by a man.

She was popular with members of her own sex. From her schooldays in North London, she had been friendly with the three daughters of a local builder. The youngest, Violet (she too was to die young, not long after marrying), was her closest companion. In February 1938 the sisters were living together in a first-floor flat in Stoke Newington, some half-dozen miles from my father's house. Knowing nothing of the tragedy, Violet and her eldest sister called the following day, a Sunday, expecting to see Doris. Stunned by the news, their tears joined my mother's. It was only when they had become calmer that Violet's experience of the previous evening was recalled and recounted.

It appeared that the two senior sisters had gone to a Saturday night dance, leaving Violet alone in the flat. Having eaten a meal, she settled down with a book. The night was cold and still, the flat in a quiet, residential road. Suddenly in the silence she heard three distinct raps on the window. Startled, but thinking there was some explanation such as a tree branch, a bird or perhaps a potential intruder, she went to the window and looked out. Seeing nothing unusual, she opened it and peered outside. There was no tree, no wind, no bird and no sign of anyone. Closing and refastening the window, she returned to her book. At once the three knocks were repeated. Now frightened, she snatched up her handbag and some other valuables, dashed into her bedroom and locked the door. When the two dance-goers returned, they were surprised by her nervousness. She told them of the knocks. They made a further inspection of the window and surroundings but found nothing to explain the sounds.

Next day at my father's house, Violet recalled that the knocks had come at about 11 p.m. My mother remembered that Doris had gone to take a bath at 10.45. The first indication that something was amiss had come when my brother, arriving home at midnight, had mentioned that the light was on in the bathroom. My mother had assumed that, having taken her bath, Doris had gone to bed. Worried, by the noisy, gas-burning geyser in the bathroom, she had instructed us never to bolt the door so that easy access would be available in emergency. On looking into the room after my brother's comment, she had found my sister lying motionless in the water.

So a strange wonderment joined our grief. The circumstances suggested that the raps on Violet's window had occurred at the very time my sister must have been dying. No such sounds had ever been heard in the flat before. But why, in the extremity of her last moments, should she have tried to signal her distress to a friend several miles distant when her brother lay sleeping a few yards away and her mother was still awake downstairs? I can only guess at an answer.

First, her innate modesty would have made her acutely aware of her nakedness. It is, therefore, logical that she would have hesitated about thinking of me for help. As to mother, their relationship had been under some stress, producing the possibility that she would not have been my sister's first thought in her crisis. No such barriers would have existed in relation to her most intimate friend.

But how could such final, desperate – and uncomprehended – sounds have been transmitted? Men of science will affirm that they could not, that such contact is impossible and that the explanation is simply a matter of coincidence, misunderstanding, malobservation or imagination. But, as history shows, men of science are not always right. And what if many such happenings take place: can they *all* be delusions? For that is the problem.

It was some time later, on reading a three-volume work by the French astronomer Camille Flammarion, that I learned of records of numerous comparable cases in which audible or visible signals had been unaccountably conveyed to close friends or relatives at the moment that individuals were expiring. The veracity of the evidence that has been accumulated in support of these phenomena is impressive. Their significance is profound, denying as they do the commonly accepted laws governing what is, and is not, thought feasible by way of communication between persons separated by distance and deprived of all normal means of contact.

Long out of print but still available at some libraries, Flammarion's treatise, *Death and Its Mystery*, spreads the quest for knowledge in these realms into areas beyond those arising from signals received at the moment of death. His first volume presents and considers a mass of similar phenomena seen and heard at widely varying periods in advance of death, while the third book covers comparable ground in respect of *post-mortem* occurrences.

The questions raised extend the inquirer's field across the entire spectrum of time and space, life and death. No one feeling a desire to examine these matters should fail to seek an early perusal of Flammarion's classical contribution.

2. The Makings

What sort of person becomes a ghost-hunter? Are such people sane? I cannot speak for others but perhaps an outline of further events in my early life will provide some basis for judgement of me.

The rural communities of Norfolk still retain some quaint attitudes and beliefs. In the years between the great wars their suspicions, superstitions, insularity and religious dogmatism were deep-rooted indeed. In those days a visitor from London was regarded almost as a creature from another planet. Money was tight and communications limited. It was by no means exceptional to meet villagers who had never visited Norwich, let alone that far-away place of low-life debauchery called the capital.

These were the surroundings into which I was sent to spend most of my school holidays. I was usually lodged with my mother's elder sister who, with her husband, lived in a hamlet called Forncett End. Aunt Agnes, precise and middle-aged, had a face like a ripened apple and a habit of noisily pursing her lips. Her existence centred upon the Primitive Methodist chapel, whither I was despatched, fiercely scrubbed and immaculately dressed, to morning Sunday School as well as being taken to evening service every sabbath of my young vacations. I hated it but there was no arguing with Aunt Agnes.

My maternal grandmother died before I was born, but my grandfather, Rayner Alexander, a burly man whose age was as great as his determination, had a small farm near Aunt Agnes' cottage. Rayner could never be persuaded to leave his home ground, even briefly. 'I don't know when my Call may come,' was his response to all invitations.

Evenings at the farm had a character all their own. There was no electricity supply. Although the power company erected poles and lines in Forncett in the mid-30s, Rayner would not have the farm connected because he feared it would set the place on fire. After dark, the ground-floor rooms were lit by ornamentally shaded paraffin lamps. The bedrooms had candles. Rayner's favourite evening place was a wooden armchair beside the well-scrubbed table in the kitchen. The lamp cast a pool of yellow light over the huge Bible, which he studied through wire-rimmed spectacles. As he read, he followed the lines with a great, blunt forefinger. And from his vast chest came the rumblings of half-uttered words. On warm nights, when the kitchen window was open, the subdued booming of his religious reading was audible across the farmyard.

But best of all, on nights when a few members of the family or friends were gathered, were the ghost stories. Many glasses of home-made cider and wine were consumed as the tales became more and more horrific. Stories of corpses seen leaving their graves, of phantom horses bearing headless riders, of hideous monsters skulking about the dark lanes. As I listened, I could feel the hairs rising on the back of my neck and shivers running down my spine. Trying not to be too obvious, I would edge closer into the comforting circle of lamplight.

The house had no indoor toilet. The closet, containing a bucket under a wooden seat, was in a small building behind the barn. Using it involved an inky-black walk on moonless nights, while moonlight produced grotesque shadows among the trees. I struggled to control my excretory functions on those tale-telling evenings. When the demands of nature could be contained no longer, I would either slip through the side door and relieve myself among the gooseberry bushes which grew just outside (once with quite painful results) or, summoning all my courage, run at breakneck speed to the toilet and back again. Ghosts, I reasoned, would not be likely to move as fast as I could.

On one occasion as I sped on my outward journey, I dashed round the corner of the barn and crashed headlong into a looming dark shape which uttered a bellow of rage. Shaking with fright, I picked myself up to run away but was instantly seized in an inescapable grip. It was the village policeman. He had decided to make use of my grandfather's toilet before inviting himself in for some cider.

The story I remember most clearly from those distant days was one told by my grandfather himself. It concerned a tree-fringed pond beside a lonely lane a mile or two from the farm. Here, it was said, a poacher had hidden in a tangle of bushes while being chased one night by a gamekeeper. To make sure of his pursuer's departure, the fugitive lay silent in the shadows for nearly an hour. All at once he heard the approach of hooves and the crunching of wheels on the gravel of the lane. Peering between the foliage, he saw a pony and cart stop beside the pond. Two men dismounted and slid out a long, heavy bundle wrapped in sacking. Each holding an end of the weighty burden, they swung it above the low roadside hedge before casting it out towards the centre of the pond. It sank with much gurgling. Because of the nature of his business, the poacher was circumspect about mentioning what he had seen. But he told a couple of trusted friends, both of whom made careful inquiries to see if some explanation could be found. They discovered nothing. Finally, the three decided to drag the pond to see if they could recover whatever it was that had been abandoned there. They were surprised by the depth of the water, which swallowed their tackle before it touched bottom. After an hour of effort, they gave up.

The story then moved to the first anniversary of the nocturnal mystery. Just before midnight a local man and his wife were walking past the pond on their way home after visiting friends. As they drew near, they became aware first of a sudden chill in the air and then of a nauseous stench. Hushing his wife's implorings that they should hurry on, the man mounted a small bank to look over the hedge into the pond, with the thought that perhaps an animal had died there and was decomposing in the water. As he gazed downwards the moon floated free of a cloud, lighting the surface like a mirror. And, as he watched, there was a sudden ripple, surrounded by spreading rings, in the centre of the pool. From that centre came a milk-white human hand whose fingers, flexing and unflexing, seemed to be grasping for some means by which to lift its possessor from the water. The man's gasping intake of breath brought his wife to his side. She too saw the awful hand just before the curling fingers ceased their empty clutching and slid back beneath the surface.

After hastily completing their journey home, the couple spent a sleepless night. Later, their story spread like wildfire. It reached the ears of the poacher who, it was said, was so frightened by it that he gave the landowner a full account of his experience – as well as abandoning his illicit activities for the remainder of his life.

My grandfather's tale ended with a description of further fruitless probings at the pond and the unrewarded efforts that were made to trace the men with the pony and cart. Finally, he assured his listeners, the dreadful hand which came groping from its watery tomb had been seen on several subsequent anniversaries when the moon's pale eye lit the face of the water. Someone asked about the date on which the spectral vision appeared. Scratching the thin grey hair above his ear, Rayner answered that it had all happened so long before that he couldn't be sure. It was, however, 'about harvest time'.

Much later, after I had learned that most fears are self-induced, I spent some night hours sitting at the edge of the pond, staring watchfully at the water. All I smelled were the night scents of the countryside; all I heard were the scurryings of nocturnal creatures; all I fancied I saw, by the moon's reflection in the pool, was my grandfather's knowing old visage, winking.

I was sent to stay with Rayner for the first school holiday following my sister's death. He had acquired a new housekeeper in the person of a bustling, grey-haired lady of well-advanced years, named Faith. Speaking with the broadest of Norfolk accents, she scampered round after my grandfather uttering dire threats as to what she would do if he didn't mend his ways. Rayner wouldn't adapt himself to her system of running the house. He wouldn't change his shirt when visitors were expected. He wouldn't let her discard the worn-out trousers in which he liked to live. Fingering the large goitre in her neck, Faith would stamp with frustration as she poured out her troubles to anyone who would listen.

Sadly, Rayner's long-awaited Call came during that holiday. He, Faith and I had lunch in the kitchen and later he went out to potter in his carefully tended garden. I stayed indoors, reading. I was startled by Faith's cries as she hurried across the yard. 'Come quick,' she yelled. 'Something's happened to your grandfather in the toilet.'

I ran to the closet, lifted the latch and tried to open the door. It moved inwards a few inches and then was stopped by something soft but unyieldingly heavy. Faith summoned two farmhands, who brought axes and broke the door from its hinges. It fell outwards, revealing my grandfather pitched forward on his purpled face, his eyes wide and staring and his trousers round his ankles. Death has no regard for dignity.

It took four men to carry him into the house, in a blanket. He was laid, under a spotless white sheet, in the room in which there had been so many story-telling evenings. Various messages were sent, including one to my parents. That night, Faith and I found ourselves alone. We retired early.

Full of imaginings from the subtle creakings of the house as its timbers cooled, I found it an exercise of will to extinguish my candle. At last I fell asleep. I am not sure whether it was the flickering of yellow light under my bedroom door or the dragging of slowly approaching feet on the bare boards of the landing that woke me in a sweat of fear. I jerked upright in bed, absolutely incapable of further movement, while the unearthly glimmer grew brighter under the ill-fitting door and the footsteps shambled closer. My mind raced. Yes, the heavy shuffling was precisely that of my grandfather. Then I caught the low mumbling of half-uttered words ...

I steeled myself for the shock of what I should see when my door was flung open. And then the flickering light began to dim and the footfalls to retreat. I breathed again – and found some courage. Without stopping to light my candle, I leapt from bed and wrenched back the door. There on the landing was the nightgowned and nightcapped Faith, her face dark-hollowed by candlelight and her absent false teeth, about to enter her bedroom.

She gave me a wan smile. 'Oi've jus' bin down to make sure yar grandad's arl roight,' she said. 'Go yow back to bed afore yow gits yar dith o' cold.'

3. Pathway Continued

My wartime years embraced an abrupt end of my formal education, marriage, fatherhood, a taste of combative nastiness, a time in hospital and the start of a career in journalism.

For a few dismal months I acted as clerk to a Gray's Inn solicitor. One morning, after an air raid, I was walking through an alleyway between tall factory buildings just off Gray's Inn Road. Many places had been blasted and burnt; debris lay everywhere. Fire-engines, pumps and rescue squads were hard at work. The alleyway narrowed and, through smashed windows, I saw that a building had been gutted to a smouldering ruin, leaving a three- or four-storey-high wall flanking the alley standing in isolation.

Suddenly a voice within me told me to stop. For a few paces I ignored it. There were many people around me, almost all walking briskly in the same direction. But the warning persisted. So, putting a foot on a pile of rubble, I pretended to tie a shoelace. At that moment, the high wall ahead collapsed into the alleyway, filling it ten feet high and burying the walkers a few yards ahead of me. Gasping in the choking dust, I helped extricate two or three people who were visible at the edge of the pile. Others could not be reached. Why was I so strangely preserved? I have no idea. There can be little doubt that people far more deserving of survival perished there.

As I reflected on it afterwards, I was reminded of a similar inner prompting when, in 1935, a radio programme was interrupted for news of the earthquake that shattered Quetta. The solemn-voiced announcer spoke of thousands of deaths, including British Army and Air Force personnel. Knowing that Ralph was stationed in the town, my mother collapsed. Doing my best to comfort her, I suddenly saw a crystal-clear picture of him, smiling and unmarked in his blue uniform. I told her I was certain all was well with him.

First inquiries at the Air Ministry produced no information. Then, a day or two later, came the confirmation – Ralph was uninjured and had volunteered to stay to help restore the broken radio station. But the number of deaths had indeed been huge. Official sources subsequently estimated the fatalities at 56,000, of whom 25,000 died in Quetta.

My 'inner voice' is a rare visitor, infrequent enough to inflict little damage on the theory that it could all be coincidence or wishful thinking. On three occasions at social functions I have known *for certain*, a few seconds in advance, that people announcing the results of raffles were about to read out the numbers of my tickets. In my work as a journalist I have experienced a form of intuition that provided me with certain advantages. One prompting took me to a Cambridgeshire village just after it had been torn apart by the accidental explosion of an ammunition train. I 'scooped' the story.

At other times the solution to pressing problems has emerged through a circuitry of slender threads. Working on a newspaper in Salisbury, Wiltshire, I endured much discomfort. The city was then home to the military of several nations; living accommodation was at a premium and went to the highest bidder. The salary of a young reporter – I was paid £6 a week – went nowhere in such a contest. My landlady ejected me from the room I had been found by my editor so that she could let it to an American serviceman at a trebled rental. For a while I enjoyed the unofficial aid of friends in the constabulary, who allowed me to occupy one of their cells. But again I was ousted, when the nightly battles that flared between British troops and others imposed capacity demands on law-enforcement premises. I found that the only lasting solution to my problem lay in volunteering for fire-guard duty in a central block of buildings. Thus, I gained the use of a camp bed, an electric kettle and a tiny allowance of tea, milk and sugar, in the office of the Inspector of Taxes.

One night, while removing incendiary bombs from the roof with the regulation long-handled shovel, I found I was being aided by an attractive female. When our work was done, she asked where I lived. On learning my plight, she insisted that I took up residence in the only place she had to offer – on a vast Chesterfield settee in the living-room of her rambling flat on the top floor. She told me she was married but had left her husband. Now, with her two toddler daughters, she was living with a slaughterman employed at a local abattoir. Sadly, what had seemed like a heaven-sent blessing soon showed its faults. The Chesterfield was exquisitely comfortable, but I had to wait until the early hours before I could occupy it. My hostess was very popular with the Americans. Jaunty young men with badge-emblazoned uniforms and gum-munching jaws sat drinking, smoking and gossiping on my 'bed' far into the night. Even then rest rarely lasted long. At seven in the morning the lady would float into the room in a filmy *néglige* and play most competently – but oh so unwelcomely – on the piano.

Her admirers showed their gratitude in material form. Supplies of meat, butter, sugar, canned fruit, liquor and even truckloads of coal – then rationed items of great scarcity on the domestic front – arrived regularly.

But lurking in the wings of this physically preoccupied scene there was a sinister 'presence'. Several times I saw previously light-hearted military guests tumble, white-faced and sobered, back to the living-room after visits to the 'usual offices' at the end of a dark corridor. While the tellers changed, the story was always the same – they had felt themselves touched by an invisible 'something' as they passed along the empty passageway.

Though I loitered in the corridor, I was never 'touched'. Yet there was an undeniable feeling of being observed by some indefinable 'presence' that drew gratification from its ability to frighten. Then a story spread among the Americans that those who were 'touched' in the corridor would not survive the war. There was a noticeable fall in the number of my hostess's military visitors and a consequent decline in her standard of living.

Not long after the return of peace I was stricken by a physical problem stemming from my wartime damage. I was not taken to hospital because, I suspect, my doctor anticipated an early and final conclusion to my difficulties.

My wife, our small son and I were then living in North London. Reading the local newspaper one afternoon, my wife drew my attention to an article describing the healing work of a woman at a Palmers Green Spiritualist centre. Would I, she asked, agree to her contacting the medium to see if she could help me? Thinking only that there was nothing to lose, I accepted the suggestion.

The following day a short, plump, animated lady of middle years walked into my bedroom and regarded me with penetrating but kindly brown eyes. Her name was Eva Rayner. She asked for no fee and refused my offer of money. For an hour she sat chatting casually to us, emitting frequent chuckles that seemed to bubble up from the soles of her feet. In that time she told us of detailed matters in our private lives which could not possibly have been known to her through normal channels. Fascinating, I thought, a really skilful telepathist. Before she left, she fixed me with a particularly piercing glance. "You will soon be well," she said. Despite my circumstances, I felt tempted to believe her.

A few weeks later I was able to get up and move around. Then, with my surprised doctor's blessing, I went back to work. Each Monday I attended the healing sessions held at Eva's little centre, a former bank she had grandly renamed *A Temple of the Trinity for Spiritual Healing*. There, aided by a small group of helpers, she dealt with sufferers who arrived throughout the day and early evening. There were no set charges. Patients placed their donations on a small offertory plate. Few gave more than a shilling or two.

Treatment required the sufferer to sit fully dressed on a chair while the healer passed her hands over head, body and limbs. Between patients, she rinsed her hands in a bowl of water. From Eva's hands as she attended me I felt a vibrant warmth which might best be described as a sensation at the opposite end of the scale from the icy resonances I later experienced at some seances and hauntings.

Brought up in the Methodist faith, Eva made it clear that her Spiritualism was based on Christianity. On Sundays the *Temple* became a chapel, with morning and evening services on the orthodox pattern except that, as well as an address, there were demonstrations of clairvoyance and clairaudience. Sometimes these were given by Eva and at others by visiting mediums. They normally began after a hymn and consisted of the placing of messages said by the sensitives to emanate from the deceased friends or relatives of people in the congregation. The substance of the messages varied. The majority were taken up with seemingly trivial references to people, places and objects. There were no profound revelations about the conditions that had been encountered after death. But most of the recipients declared themselves convinced of the survival of their loved ones because of the details they were given. It was apparent that, perhaps because of bereavement and loneliness, many were pathetically credulous.

Eva's mediumistic abilities never emerged as strongly at her public demonstrations as they did when she gave private sittings. Over the years I enjoyed a number of solo seances at her home in Southgate, sometimes at her invitation and sometimes at my own request. They were memorable because of her physical performance as well as their mental impact. Eva declared that on these occasions, as during her healing work, she became an instrument of communication between the living world and the spirit of a former Carmarthen medical practitioner, a Dr Lewis, who had died on 6 February 1902, aged eighty-six. She affirmed that she had been able to trace the details of the doctor's earthly life and professional career from information he had provided during seances.

Sitting upright, she would close her eyes and, with a few slight shudders, apparently sink into cataleptic trance. Straightening from the knees, which always projected clear of the edge of the chair, her legs would stick out horizontally, unsupported. She would remain in this position throughout the sittings, which usually lasted for between forty minutes and an hour. Unlike some mediums whose 'trance-state' voices assume tones appropriate to the entities they claim as spirit guides, Eva spoke almost normally, except for a little gruffness, during her seances. There was rarely one that failed to impress me with the depth of understanding revealed about my background, my family and forebears and, indeed, my private thoughts and ambitions. Even allowing for her growing personal knowledge of me, there was invariably a nucleus of information she could not have acquired by ordinary means. There were also predictions, many of which have been fulfilled.

When I questioned her about her sensations during trance, she told me she knew nothing of what she said while in that state. 'As I go under, I simply feel I am falling asleep.' And, typical of her humour, 'Sister Wilkin [her constant companion, a retired hospital sister who said she had been cured of Meniere's disease by Eva's ministrations] used to have to watch me like a hawk because at first I had an intense urge to take my teeth out as I was going!' Other mediums with whom I discussed their bodily reactions to trance reported that their feelings ranged from total unconsciousness to a slight daze during which words 'enter my mind' and were spoken without the filtration of thought.

But the examination of Spiritualistic phenomena, related though they may be to the 'spontaneous' happenings encountered in hauntings, is another study. With insufficient space here for both subjects, I must concentrate on the latter and leave the former for another volume.

4. Things That Go Bump

The aspiring ghost-hunter should find little difficulty in discovering material for investigation. Every year newspapers carry many stories of alleged encounters with the paranormal. Some tell of strange sightings, others of unaccountable sounds. But by far the most frequent are reports of the depredations of the ever-ubiquitous poltergeist.

Records of these disturbances extend far into the past in many lands, but it was in Germany that the now generally accepted name was first applied: *polter*, the making of noise, and *geist*, spirit. Thus 'Noisy spirit'.

Early documentation detailing the exploits of these riotous intruders is not easy to trace, in part no doubt because the victims were not always able to place blame where it belonged. There is certainly reason to believe that poltergeist infestation may have been the true explanation of some of the incidents that led to the agonized ends of poor wretches done to death during the hideous barbarities of the fifteenth-, sixteenth- and seventeenth-century witchhunts in Europe and America. During the eighteen years from 1643 to 1661, some four thousand hapless creatures were painfully executed for 'witchcraft' in Britain. In Salem, Massachusetts, even a dog was hanged during a similar wave of hysterical injustice. With this bloody past, it may not be altogether correct to continue repeating the oft-quoted statement that the poltergeist has never brought serious physical injury to any human being.

But what do poltergeists do? Describing some of my inquiries in a 'seasonal account of ghosts' for a December 1955 issue of *Everybody's Weekly*, the well-known novelist and historian James Laver wrote:

The dictionaries translate the German word poltergeist as hobgoblin, and for most English people hobgoblins belong to the nursery, shut firmly now and forever within the pages of *Grimm's Fairy Tales*. But the poltergeist refuses to be shut up in this manner. He is with us today ... a noisy sprite who makes his presence felt by banging, knocking, and throwing things about.

Most people today would dismiss this as nonsense. There are no poltergeists, and all the stories about them spring from credulity or deliberate fraud. Unfortunately, this theory won't hold water.

Anyone who has had the curiosity to look into the matter in anything but the most superficial way is compelled to admit that the weight of evidence for their existence and activities is overwhelming.

The poltergeist is a troublesome fellow in the world of mind as well as in the world of events. He is no 'grey lady' or headless knight moving in stately fashion down the corridors of some ancestral mansion. He seems to choose his scene of operations quite arbitrarily. Often, but not always, it is some lonely cottage. His manifestations – his bag of tricks – seem singularly limited.

And there is nearly always an adolescent present, usually a girl with whose emotional disturbance the whole strange business seems to be mixed up, but in a way nobody can understand.

Ah! say the sceptics, that is what the lawyers would call a very damaging admission. There is always a young person present in a state of emotional disturbance. Such persons are only too anxious to draw attention to themselves. The whole thing is trickery.

It is certainly true that in several cases trickery has been discovered. But many phenomena cannot be explained away.

One of the strangest and most carefully investigated cases was reported in the *Atlantic Monthly* in 1868. An Irish servant girl was employed by a family in Massachusetts, and six weeks after she came into service all the bells in the house began ringing violently. The wires were detached but they continued to ring.

The family saw them agitated without cause, for although the girl was in the room with them they were watching her closely and, in any case, the bells were hung some 11 feet high, near the ceiling. A heavy stone slab weighing 48 pounds, on which the girl was placing a tea-tray, suddenly flew up, struck the tray and upset the dishes on it.

Later, while she was wringing some clothes, it jumped up again and fell back with such force that it broke in two. It is difficult to see how this could have been accomplished by the girl even if there had been no-one watching her. But the author of the article in the *Atlantic Monthly* states that he was present at the time.

Sir William Barrett, FRS, was able to investigate in person the strange happenings in a hamlet called Derrygonnelly, near Enniskillen, in Ireland, in 1877. He took with him a learned Dublin clergyman named the Rev Maxwell Close, one of the earliest members of the Society for Psychical Research.

It is impossible to believe that these two gentlemen were lying and yet the story they tell is certainly a strain on our credulity. For when they had satisfied themselves that everybody in the house was accounted for, or with them in the kitchen, raps were heard increasing in loudness all round the place. Barrett rapped himself and the poltergeist rapped back.

'Then' (in Sir William's own words) 'I mentally asked it, no word being spoken, to knock a certain number of times and it did so. To avoid any error or delusion on my part, I put my hands in the pockets of my overcoat and asked it to knock the number of fingers I had open. It correctly did so. Then, with a different number of fingers open each time, the experiment was repeated four times in succession, and four times I obtained the correct number of raps.'

How often do these extraordinary things occur? Not very often perhaps but there are nonetheless enough cases to amount to a formidable body of evidence. Some of them have become sufficiently famous to merit the word 'classic'. Perhaps the best known of all is that of Epworth Rectory.

Epworth is in a remote part of Lincolnshire and in the early years of the eighteenth century the rectory was inhabited by the Wesley family. The very name is sufficient to command attention and respect. John Wesley himself had already left home when the manifestations began, but he was sufficiently interested to obtain from almost every member of the household a written statement; he collected these, collated them carefully and published them.

Among them are long and detailed letters from his redoubtable mother. Even the most confirmed sceptic is hardly likely to affirm that Susannah Wesley was a liar or a fool. Nor was her husband, the Rev Samuel Wesley, who set down in his diary 'An Account of Noises and Disturbances in my House at Epworth, Lincolnshire, in December and January, 1716.'

They began with knockings under the feet, groans and the noise of bottles being broken, footsteps and the sound of 'gobbling like a turkey-cock'. There was a sound 'like the strong winding up of a jack'. The latches of doors were lifted up.

'One night,' wrote the Rev Wesley, 'when the noise was great in the kitchen, and on a deal partition, and on the door in the yard, the latch whereof was often lifted up, my daughter Emilia went and held it fast on the inside, but it was still lifted up, and the door pushed violently against her, though nothing was to be seen on the outside.'

But, the sceptic will cry, all this is a very long time ago. What then ... about the famous Borley Rectory, publicised as 'the most haunted house in England'? The famous psychic investigator Harry Price actually rented the place for a year and invited people to study the matter with him.

Among the forty who were accepted as collaborators was Professor Joad, who duly spent a night in the house and wrote an account of his experience in *Harper's Magazine* for July 1938.

Professor Joad began by being extremely sceptical, but in the end found it 'equally impossible to withhold credence from the facts or to credit any possible explanation of the facts. Either the facts did not occur, or if they did, the universe must in some respects be totally other than what one is accustomed to suppose.'

Later Borley Rectory was completely destroyed by fire as if the poltergeist – they are notorious incendiaries – were tired of being investigated.

Recently Philip Paul has taken up the matter again. In case Price's testimony should not be enough to carry conviction, he was careful to obtain statements from witnesses who had nothing to do with Price. Price first went to Borley in 1929 and died in 1948.

Paul chose his witnesses from those who were able to report phenomena from 1900, from the period between 1916 and 1920 and from the years 1949 and 1955. All this adds up to a formidable amount of evidence which it is very difficult to explain away.

5. My Work at Haunted Borley

It was not without reason that Laver's article raised an implied question about the adequacy of Price's testimony on Borley. It was known that three senior members of the Society for Psychical Research were preparing a report aimed at showing that Price had concocted some of the strange incidents described in his two widely sold books on the case.

For the reader new to the story, a brief summary of the history may be helpful. The torrent of words written and spoken about strange events in the remote hamlet tucked away on the Suffolk/Essex border began in earnest in 1940, with publication of Price's *The Most Haunted House in England*. The apparent durability of the phenomena and the success of the book were reflected in the appearance, six years later, of a second work by the same author – *The End of Borley Rectory*.

Then, a decade on, Eric Dingwall, Kathleen Goldney and Trevor Hall produced, under the auspices of the Society for Psychical Research, a report entitled *The Haunting of Borley Rectory*. It set out not only to demolish the evidence assembled by Price but also to show that Price himself had resorted to fraud to keep the case alive. Freed of the legal inhibitions relating to defamation – Price died in 1948 and the libel laws afford no protection to the dead – the report caused a sensation with its aim of debunking the great debunker. Price was accused of manufacturing some of the effects his books had presented as paranormal, of falsifying his accounts of other incidents and of deceiving honest and reputable aides into believing the haunting to be genuine. After referring to his 'cynical misrepresentation', the vengeful trio declared, 'When analysed, the evidence for haunting and poltergeist activity for each and every period appears to diminish in force and finally to vanish away.'

Price's accusers were not undivided for long. Two years after publication of *The Haunting of Borley Rectory* there was a major squabble between them following the appearance of another work, by Dingwall and Hall, again assailing the reputation of Dingwall's lifelong rival, Price. Called *Four Modern Ghosts*, the book accused Price of fabricating his account of the so-called 'Rosalie seance', an event at which, he said, he believed he had handled the materialized nude body of a six-year-old girl in a house in South London.

At that time friendly with Price, Goldney had recorded that she had found him pale, exhausted and 'shaken to the core by his experience' the morning after his 'Rosalie' sitting. Dingwall and Hall published her stated impressions of his post-seance condition in *Four Modern Ghosts*, adding: 'It will be obvious to the reader that one objection to the hypothesis that the Rosalie story was wholly or mainly fictitious rests on the testimony of Mrs Goldney.' Furious, the lady informed the Spiritualist weekly *Two Worlds* that her co-authors in *The Haunting of Borley Rectory* had not told her there was to be a new attack on Price. Her first knowledge of *Four Modern Ghosts* had come after the book had been published, when *Two Worlds* asked for her comments. She recalled that Hall had written asking her to provide him with details of her meeting with Price the day after the 'Rosalie' seance, but had not mentioned that her recollections were to be used in another onslaught on the departed psychist. 'If they wanted to know whether I thought Price had fabricated his account, why didn't they ask me? I would have answered "After Borley I lost faith in him, but I don't believe he invented this Rosalie story",' *Two Worlds* quoted her as saying.

Price's detractors on Borley did not go unchallenged. One of the sequels was a studiously compiled dissection of their indictment by another member of the SPR, Robert Hastings. Published in 1969, it was modestly titled *An Examination of the 'Borley Report'*.

It is not my purpose to reopen the controversy concerning Price. It has been argued back and forth, orally and in writing, *ad nauseam*. What I do believe worth restating is the primary point I made in newspaper articles following the Dingwall/Goldney/Hall attack: that, even were the whole of Price's work at Borley to be utterly and finally dismissed, the case for paranormalities having occurred there would remain unscathed. The SPR authors' assertion, 'When analysed, the evidence for haunting and poltergeist activity for each and every period appears to diminish in force and finally to vanish away', was an insupportable overstatement. Let me explain.

Price first heard of Borley on 11 June 1929 and first visited the place the following day. He died, aged sixty-seven, on 29 March

1948. During my early inquiries at Borley I gathered evidence, from reliable witnesses, of sightings of the 'nun' phantasm and other unexplained happenings in 1900, 1916–19, 1927, 1949, 1953 and 1955 – all years before and after Price's involvement. Unlike Price's interviews, mine were conducted with the techniques of a journalist experienced in questioning individuals ranging from bishops to burglars. Also differing from Price's methods – and those of other amateur interrogators who arrived on the scene – my examinations were recorded on the spot, in verbatim shorthand.

Price was a good storyteller but a bad reporter. Most of his writing on Borley was composed from notes he made from memory after driving over 150 miles back to his Sussex home and sometimes after intervals of several days. I soon learned, from people who pointed out gross errors in the accounts Price ascribed to them, that his books were by no means free of inaccuracy.

I must add the observation that allegations are always facilitated by picking on items which suit the argument and ignoring those that don't. The cursory reader would be impressed by the *prima facie* case presented by Dingwall, Goldney and Hall. Closer examination is necessary to detect the 'inconvenient' elements that were omitted. Anyone with the time and inclination to compare Price's Borley books (allowing for their imperfections) detail for detail with the work of the SPR authors will have little trouble in recognizing that the latter was prepared with careful selectivity.

The anti-Price bibliography includes another work, published in 1978. This time, the trio of critics which had previously shrunk to two was reduced still further, to one – Trevor Hall. A surveyor by trade, Hall had evidently spent much time on further efforts to prise damaging skeletons out of Price's personal cupboard. Oddly, he called his solo effort *Search for Harry Price*. With obvious relish he declared that Price's claims about his origin and education were false. Price had, said Hall, stated that he was the son of a wealthy manufacturer and had been educated at Shrewsbury. Instead, his father had been an unsuccessful grocer, he had been educated in South London, had worked as a commercial traveller selling glue and had acquired the money that enabled him to devote his time to psychical research and other pursuits by marrying an heiress.

The *Times Literary Supplement* reviewer Arthur Calder-Marshall commented that Hall and Archdeacon Charles Ellison (who contributed an essay attacking Price's standing as a numismatist) had 'left unturned no stone that might hide a dirty secret. But they have made no attempt to explore the climate of Harry Price's life.'

So much for Price. Now what of Borley?

The strange occurrences reported between the years 1900 and 1960 included:

Repeated sightings of a phantasm with the appearance of a nun
A phantom coach and horses
A ghostly dog
The unaccountable movement of objects
The throwing of stones
Inexplicable crashes, raps, taps, thumps, knockings and scratchings
'Dragging' sounds
Whisperings
Footsteps
The ringing of bells whose operating wires had been cut
Miscellaneous poltergeist-type disturbances
Odd odours – pleasant and unpleasant
Wall-writings
Spontaneous outbreaks of fire
A localized 'cold spot'
Unaccountable door locking and unlocking
Strange lights in windows
Organ playing in the locked and empty church

The majority of the phenomena were observed in and around the rectory, a spacious house built in 1863 for the Reverend Henry Dawson Ellis Bull, the comfortably-off incumbent, who fathered fourteen children and added a wing to his home to accommodate his expanding family. From time to time, extraordinary incidents were also reported in and near the tiny twelfth-century church across the lane, these apparently increasing after the main rectory building was gutted by fire in 1939 and finally demolished in 1944.

Visiting Borley soon after Price's death, I made the acquaintance of the then Rector of Borley-cum-Liston, the Reverend Alfred Henning, and his charming, erudite wife, Eva. It was the beginning of a warm friendship during which I received much help and hospitality. Living at the more moderately proportioned Liston Rectory – they had been daunted by the 'overpowering, vast and ugly' house at Borley when Henning took up the joint incumbency in 1936 – they accommodated me several times in their home and provided detailed information about the locality and their personal experiences in Borley Rectory and church.

Receiving the bishop's permission to put the unwanted rectory up for sale, the quiet and reticent Henning found difficulty in disposing of the inconvenient edifice. He was, therefore, happy to accept Price's offer to rent the place for a year from May 1937. Advertising in *The Times* for voluntary helpers, Price organized a twelve-month surveillance of the premises by a rota of forty-eight part-time observers. Accounts of the strange happenings they witnessed were recorded in Price's *Most Haunted House.* Some of their reports, Price's handling of them and his directions for the year-long watch were sternly attacked in *The Haunting of Borley Rectory.*

In their criticism of the descriptions of inexplicable footsteps heard in the house, the SPR authors suggested that these were all due to hallucination, the presence of intruders who had gained entry through the well and cellars or the reflected sounds of normal human movements in the tenanted rectory cottage 'not 25 feet away'. The validity of such views may be judged from Henning's own account of events one evening in July 1937, when he and his wife joined one of Price's helpers, Mark Kerr-Pearse, in the small, ground-floor library room facing onto the large, wide-lawned garden. It is taken from a booklet, *Haunted Borley*, published by Henning in 1948.

> As we went in I carefully put the chain up at the front door, and I want to make it quite clear that we took every precaution to prevent anyone playing tricks on us. All the doors and windows were locked and sealed. The only entrance was the French window of the small study where we sat talking at a table. In so far as it was humanly possible we had made sure that there was no way in or out of the rectory except by that window.
>
> There is little doubt, I fancy, that at such times when one is keyed up to a pitch, the slightest noise makes an impression. And the odd thing about the rectory, a fact I had noticed repeatedly since my first day inside it, was the abnormal quiet of the place. *One had the idea that the vast block of masonry somehow protected you from the outside sounds and acted as proof against them.* [My italics.] In a short time, the creaking of boards shrinking after dark in the cool of the night no longer disturbed you but, on a night such as this, I believe anyone who had sat with us would have been more than usually aware of anything out of the ordinary.
>
> It was getting dusk. Mr Kerr-Pearse was, if I remember, telling us of a conversation he had had with one of the villagers that morning, when there was a noise of someone opening a door. We sat and waited in silence and I can remember myself thinking how bright the light of the lamp was

> and that it needed turning down before it began to flare. [The rectory had no supply of mains electricity, gas or water] I suppose subconsciously I was very glad to have that lamp there. If my eyes were fixed upon it, my ears and those of my companions were on the passage outside and the door which had opened. All of us had heard it. As for me, a curious pricking sensation came over me and when, afterwards, I told my wife of it, she said she had had the same sensation, coupled with a fear not of anything paranormal but of what she was going to see, and that something, she said, might be horrible. You must remember that we three were alone in the study, in the house, with only a door between us and what had emerged from another door in the passage outside.
>
> And then, in the utter quiet of the night, we could hear footsteps *coming up the long stone-flagged passage leading from the kitchen quarters* [my italics] and with the steps and, as it were, following after them, came a swishing noise as of long trailing garments. We rose slowly from our seats and still continued, in the frightening silence penetrated only by those footsteps, to wait. The whole house, the difference in our personalities, the very idea that we were impartial investigators who were supposed to be above being swept away by any emotion of any kind, were absorbed and concentrated into those footsteps where no footsteps should be, that opening door and swishing garments in a house we knew to be empty ... *They came down the long passage nearer and nearer to the study.* [My italics.] Our bodies were tensed as if to ward off a blow and I had become, suddenly, thirsty.
>
> When we could stand the tension no longer we went to the door and opened it. I do not know who actually opened it or suggested going to the door. Nothing had been said but it was as if we were not three separate people, but one. All I remember was that I had a feeling of not being able to listen any longer to those steps and the next moment we, all three of us, were at the door. Without a word, we ran into the passage and looked about us to see – nothing. *The moment the door opened the sounds ceased* [my italics] and the two nightlights, which had been placed in the passage, were still burning brightly.

The italicized phrases need to be examined against the Dingwall, Goldney and Hall assertion that all the footsteps heard in the house could be accounted for by imagination, intruders or the cottage tenants walking about their home. It was true that the occupants of the library were 'not 25 feet away' from the cottage – they were three times that distance from the entirely detached building, on the other side of two stout and well-separated external and several indirectly intervening internal walls.

The next question must be whether Henning was hallucinated or lying. Knowing him as I did, as a devout and transparently honest seeker for truth, I have no doubt about the answer. If there was hallucination, it must have applied, simultaneously, to three intelligent and responsible individuals. As to falsehood, this would have been as foreign to Henning as belief in Spiritualism is to most psychical researchers.

Henning reported a number of strange happenings in and around the church. The first occurred in April 1942. It had been his practice to keep a small sanctuary lamp burning day and night near the tabernacle, as an indication that the sacrament was reserved for cases of emergency, but during the war it was noticed that the light could be seen at night from some distance down the hill. Thereafter, a church helper living nearby extinguished the lamp at dusk and relit it each morning. For almost two weeks she found that the small wick was removed from the lamp in the locked church during the night. To stop this, a weighty psalter and other covers were placed over the lamp each evening. On three occasions they were found scattered on the floor. Although a mouse was later caught in the church, Henning commented, 'I cannot think so small a creature could have upset the heavy psalter in this way.'

One Sunday when a party of local children arrived as usual for their catechism class and were sitting near the organ awaiting the arrival of their teacher, they heard footsteps enter the porch and the key turn in the lock. Running to the door and finding it fastened, one of the children called out 'We are here, Miss Byford.' There was absolute silence. The children became alarmed at finding themselves prisoners in the building, but a few minutes later their teacher, Miss Byford, arrived – and was astonished to find the door locked from the outside. Suspecting a practical joke, Henning made some discreet enquiries but found no evidence. 'In view of all that has happened in the porch since then, I think the locking of the door was a paranormal experience,' he wrote.

Another incident, in which he was personally involved, occurred late one summer afternoon when he was showing Harry Price the newly restored mensa. Standing talking in the chancel, they were suddenly interrupted by loud and prolonged screeching from rooks inhabiting the elms around the church. When the noise died down, footsteps were heard in the porch. Regretting that his talk with Price was to be disturbed, Henning waited for someone to appear. No one did. Hurrying to the door and going quickly through the churchyard, he looked up and down the road. There was nobody in sight. 'Anyone playing a trick would not have had time to disappear before I caught them,' Henning stated. A few days later, when he was visiting the church with two young friends, the bird-screeching, footsteps in the porch and unsuccessful search were repeated.

In the autumn, a novelist friend asked Henning to show her the restored altar. They drove to the church at 3 p.m. Walking through the churchyard, both heard the sound of the organ – 'quite loud, as if someone was playing a voluntary before a service'. Hurrying ahead, the rector noted that the sounds stopped as he entered the porch. Inside, all was still and deserted, the organ keyboard locked as usual. 'It would have been impossible for anyone to get away as we approached, for the only two doors faced us as we came along the path. Moreover, the organ requires a blower,' Henning noted. Walking repeatedly up and down the church path, he and his guest listened carefully for anything they might have mistaken for organ music. The only sounds were of two tractors and a distant aeroplane. Speculating on the possibility of imagination, Henning wrote: 'In talking the matter over afterwards, we both agreed that the thought of the organ playing had not occurred to either of us on the way to the church, but we had both wondered if we might hear footsteps.'

On several occasions Henning and others experienced the apparently paranormal movement of objects in the church while they were present in the building.

He was by no means an instinctive or total supporter of preternatural explanations.

> I myself believe that the spiritual bodies of the departed do appear at times to people [he wrote in his booklet], but I should not care to claim this is so with regard to the Borley nun. Incidentally, I may remark here that there is much confused thinking over the natural and the spiritual body. St Paul's clear teaching that we have two bodies, the natural and spiritual, has either been forgotten or ignored. In so far as people have thought of Resurrection at all, they have thought of it almost wholly in terms of the natural body. I suppose it is conceivable that a spiritual body might be so earthy (I use St Paul's own term) as to be earthbound for a long period.
>
> I have been frequently asked to hold a Requiem Mass for the nun. I hold it a grievous omission to neglect prayers for the departed, but I do not feel I could hold a service for a being whose identity is so shadowy.

Dealing with the question 'Is Borley haunted?', he commented that the triviality of many of the phenomena seemed to him to indicate their genuineness. With few exceptions, he believed trickery could be ruled out:

> In all these years ... no one has come forward as a 'joker' and I fancy it a poor reward for his ingenuity to remain anonymous for so long. Generally, such people reveal themselves, if only to be praised for their cleverness!
>
> Take, for example, the footsteps in the church. Can we suppose on the evidence that they are in any way connected with the vision of the nun ... ? It is impossible to say, but I feel that the day Mr Price and I dug in the cellars of the old rectory and discovered the remains of a female jawbone [August 1943] may have some connection with the nun.

Giving his views on attempts to communicate with the dead, he observed: 'I would say a word on seances, often claimed as a means of finding out what a spirit requires of us. The answers given are quite contradictory and may arise from the subconscious mind. I, myself, place no reliance on seances and, indeed, consider them wrong in principle.'

A footnote appended to this paragraph read: 'When Mr Brown, who was kindly typing my manuscript, reached the point recording my disapproval of seances, the small hand lamp near him was suddenly swept from the table by some invisible force. He neither shook the table nor touched the lamp. He demonstrated to me exactly what happened and told me he had been typing with the lamp in the same position for weeks past.' 'Mr Brown' was, in fact, a pseudonym for James Turner, a well-known writer who was then owner of the rectory site and cottage and who had asked Henning not to identify him in this connection.

For reasons already given, I do not propose to add further to the existing mountain of words about events at Borley during the nineteen years of Price's involvement, from 1929 to 1948. As I have said, the case does not rest solely upon the happenings – be they genuine or fraudulent – of that period.

Foremost among the witnesses of the Borley phenomena was Ethel Bull, a daughter of the cleric who had the house constructed. I spent many hours in her company at her home at Great Cornard, some four miles from Borley, and heard again and again the remarkable story she had to tell. Never was she guilty of the least contradiction or discrepancy in any of her clear and concise accounts. Gently gripping my hand as I sat beside her on her sofa one afternoon, she put a simple question: 'What would be the use of an old lady like me, waiting to meet her Maker, telling a lot of fairy stories?'

An octogenarian when I first met her, she demonstrated a physical energy and mental acuity that belied her years. The one faculty that was beginning to fail her was her eyesight. Small and wiry of build and usually to be found in her garden wearing tweeds and Wellington boots, with a hairnet over her silver locks, she shared her house with her brother Alfred, a bent and gnome-like figure whose gruff response to questions about the Borley oddities was always the same: 'I never saw or heard a thing.'

It was, Ethel Bull told me, on the sunny afternoon of 28 July 1900 that she first saw the ghostly 'nun'. She was returning from a local garden party, accompanied by two of her sisters. The three girls entered the extensive rectory garden by the gate furthest from the house. Almost at once, all three saw 'a dark, female figure, dressed like a nun' gliding towards a small stream that bisected the garden about halfway along its length. The figure was some distance away from them; no facial features were discernible, nor any lighter colouration about the garments. In a time and place where strangers were few, there was something weird about the shape and its motion. The girls were frightened. Two stopped in their tracks to watch while the third ran to the house and summoned a fourth sister who, although she saw the figure, refused to believe there was anything inexplicable about it and moved to intercept – whereupon the phantom halted and then abruptly vanished.

'Clever' words like 'hallucination' and 'hypnotism' have been bandied about in attempts to rationalize this remarkable collective experience, in most cases with scanty, if any, conception of how such explanations might apply. Ethel was scornful of them all. 'We had never been hypnotized, we were not imaginative and we were certainly not drunk,' she told me with the matter-of-fact down-to-earthness of the lifelong countrywoman. She had carefully described what she had seen to each of the other girls, Freda, Mabel and Elsie, and it was obvious that they had all witnessed the presence, movements and instant disappearance of the same figure.

Singly and in pairs, the sisters saw the same apparition on several subsequent occasions. In November 1900 Ethel Bull and the family cook saw the figure leaning over a gate.

As no one has ever traced the existence of a convent (or a monastery) at Borley, the appellation 'nun' is gratuitous. Eva Henning had a theory that the ghost might have been that of Frances Waldegrave, the widow of Sir Edward, who died in the Tower of

London in 1561 during imprisonment for celebrating Roman Catholic Mass at Borley contrary to the laws of the period. At first buried at the Tower, his body was later reinterred at Borley where, in 1599, it was joined by that of Frances. The family's prominence in the area – Sir Edward was a descendant of Sir Richard Waldegrave, a Speaker of the House of Commons – is indicated by the scale of the Waldegrave tomb in Borley church. The widow's weeds of the time, Eva pointed out, were not dissimilar to the attire of a nun. But records show that the bereaved Frances remarried.

Ethel Bull also described some strange experiences inside the rectory. One night she awoke with a start to see a figure of a tall, dark man, sombrely dressed and wearing a tall hat, standing beside her bed. When she leapt up in alarm, the figure vanished. On two other occasions she had been convinced that someone – or something – was sitting on her bed, although she could see no intruder.

She died in 1961, aged ninety-three and still sticking to her story.

Other important pre-Price witnesses at Borley were Mr and Mrs Edward Cooper, a stolid and unimaginative rural working-class couple who shied away from describing their experiences because of the local ridicule that invariably followed publicity. I talked with them on several occasions at their Sudbury home, going into great detail about the happenings they reported. Again there was absolute consistency in their accounts, with firm correction of one of Price's errors.

Cooper was groom-gardener to the Bull family from 1916 to 1920. He and his wife occupied the rooms above the coach house which, converted into a cottage, later became the sole remnant of the nineteenth-century structures on the site. During their years there, the Coopers suffered repeated outbreaks of poltergeist phenomena, the most regular of which were nocturnal sounds of pattering, like the feet of a large dog. Once they were disturbed by a black, dwarf-like figure which rushed round their bed before disappearing. On another occasion, just as they were falling asleep, there was what Mrs Cooper described as 'a great crash from my kitchen. It was very loud and I thought all my crockery had been smashed.' Dashing from their bed, they made an instant inspection. To their amazement, nothing was displaced or damaged.

Clearly embarrassed by the apparent *naïveté* of his story but declaring it to be the unvarnished truth – like Ethel Bull, he asked what, at his advanced age, he had to gain by lying – Cooper told me of the moonlit night when, looking out of his bedroom window, he saw a black coach, drawn by a pair of bay horses and complete with glittering brass lamps and harness, sweep soundlessly into the rectory courtyard and there vanish. At the time, his employer kept only a brougham and a single horse. Only the vehicle was housed in the space beneath Cooper's home, the animal being stabled in a separate building. In his *Most Haunted House*, Price reported that this sighting was 'in the meadow by the church opposite', but Cooper told me that he had been looking out from the rear of the cottage, in the opposite direction to that specified by Price, when he saw the spectacle.

Cooper also described a sighting of the 'nun' phantasm in daylight. He said he watched it for several seconds while it moved silently through the garden and entered the house.

Avoiding the 'Price period', we now make a jump of thirty years – to August 1949.

Driving past the rectory garden, up the gentle hill towards the church, one warm afternoon in that month, middle-aged Dr Margaret Abernethy, a general medical practitioner based in nearby Long Melford, was intent on professional thoughts – she was *en route* to visit a patient living at Borley Green – when she noticed a nun stooping amid the tall weeds and grass growing in the disused and wired-up gateway to the rectory site. As she passed, the nun looked up and smiled, giving the doctor a clear view of her face. Dr Abernethy mentally noted her age as 'about forty'. The figure appeared perfectly normal in every respect.

Having travelled a short distance past the gateway, the doctor remembered that the nearest convent was some three miles away. The weather was oppressive, not providing comfortable conditions for walking. Thinking that a lift might be acceptable, she reversed back to the gateway she had passed only seconds earlier. To her surprise, the nun had vanished. Puzzled, she made an immediate search of the surroundings, looking in the rectory garden, in the field opposite and along the straight road. There was nowhere for anyone to hide – but there was no longer any nun.

Giving me the above account of her experience, the plump, curly grey-haired medico included a laughing reference to the reactions she expected from her male medical colleagues in the district. 'I know exactly what they will say when they hear about it,' she chuckled. 'Their only comment will be "Another menopausal woman!" I really don't care. I saw what I saw and there's an end of it.'

When the tall weeds in the gateway were being cut a week or two after her strange sighting, an old rosary was found deep in the grass.

As might be thought appropriate in a locality originally named Boarlea – 'the place of the pig' – Mr and Mrs Robert Bacon purchased the rectory cottage and site from James Turner in 1951. They moved in with their two young children, a son, Terry, and a daughter, Jose, and Mrs Bacon's parents, Mr and Mrs Henry Williams. A sociable family group, they brought a healthy scepticism to their famous surroundings. Bob Bacon came from a Norfolk farming background; his father-in-law was a retired engineer.

Shortly after their arrival Williams was working in the paved yard behind the cottage one afternoon, repairing some chicken coops. As he moved about selecting pieces of wood, nails and tools, he heard footsteps following him. Thinking it was his son-in-law, he opened a conversation. There was no response. Swinging round to remonstrate with Bob for his rudeness, Williams found he was alone. 'But there was no mistaking the footsteps,' he told me. 'They were loud and distinct, and I am certain I did not imagine them.'

Two years later he had an experience reminiscent of the 'nun' phantom. Working at a bench just below a window in an outhouse in August 1953 (the prevalence of curious incidents during summer months has been a noticeable feature of the Borley phenomena), his attention was suddenly caught by something passing by outside. Looking up, he saw moving past the window the head and shoulders of a black-clad figure, a cowl-like headdress obscuring the facial profile. He made an immediate search of the surrounding area but found nothing.

His grandson Terry, a hardworking, responsible and uncomplicated boy nearing his teens, claimed to have seen the 'nun' three times in his first four years at Borley. On two occasions, he said, the figure was in the churchyard, and both times it was floating three or four feet clear of the ground. These sightings had been from his bedroom window. Trying to explain this phenomenon, theorists said that the prolonged medieval practice of piling uncoffined corpses one upon the other had raised some churchyards several feet above normal level; it was not until the late 1800s that a tidying-up restored former surfaces. Was it possible that the Borley 'nun' had been 'walking' on ground where she had known it to be in her lifetime?

Terry's mother, Betty, claimed that she experienced several instances of paranormally moved objects in the house. Sometimes, she said, household articles would disappear altogether for a period, then equally mysteriously return. This inconsequential prank-playing was apparently not confined within the building. Walking in the garden one still and windless morning, she said, she was astonished to see a tall weed of the type known in East Anglia as 'sheeps' parsley' suddenly bend over as though bowing to her approach, touching its clusters of small white flowers to the ground. Having completed this movement, it sprang upright once more. Apart from the unexplained motion, the plant's undamaged restoration to the vertical was itself extraordinary, since any bending of that type of weed almost always snaps the brittle stem.

Her mother, Mrs Williams, who was in a delicate state of health, was distressed by an experience which befell her as she strolled on the garden path known as 'the Nun's Walk'. As she moved slowly along, she was pursued by sounds like the noisy panting of a dog. No dog was present, and no explanation could be found.

The family said they witnessed numerous unaccountable raps, knocks and 'luminous glows' in the house. Some of these may have been minor manifestations of the poltergeist phenomenon that is sometimes connected with children at puberty – or, indeed, have been due to normal juvenile mischief – rather than having any association with the Borley mysteries. Apart from their natural children, the Bacons adopted two others.

Mrs Williams died in 1959. Having sold the cottage and rectory site for some £15,000 (in 1938 the undamaged rectory, cottage, outbuildings and over three acres of land had been bought for £500!) in 1972 the family moved to Great Cornard, where Williams died a few months later.

In the late summer of 1954, after careful consideration of information provided to me from an authoritative source, I was persuaded of the desirability of arranging a systematic subterranean exploration of the rectory site. Nothing of the kind had been attempted before, earlier digging having been confined to brief efforts in the wells and cellars. Henning, Price and some helpers recovered parts of a human female skull and jawbone in August 1943.

Because of approaching autumn, there was no time to be lost. I sought, and was kindly given, the owners' permission to carry out major digging operations on the site. News of my intentions soon reached the Press and my telephone was kept busy with their calls. Having been told that labour was not easily obtained in the area because of the late harvest, I took the opportunity to intimate that volunteer helpers would be welcome so long as they were willing to provide their own transport and sustenance. Considerable correspondence and other preparations followed.

Before starting operations I made careful measurements among the tangled undergrowth to determine the points at which the first holes needed to be dug. Apart from a piece of rusty machinery, set in concrete, marking the site of the principal well, nothing of the rectory building remained above ground. Using the well as an anchor point and working from detailed plans of the former house, I first marked the place coinciding with the mysterious first-floor 'cold spot', followed by two other places of theoretical promise within the cellar area.

Work then began. I had engaged two local labourers, named Sandford and Richardson. I was also greatly aided by two volunteer helpers, Leonard Sewell, a photographer's assistant, of Long Melford, and Leonard Rayner, of Ipswich. Sewell provided me with an excellent photographic record of the work and acted as my deputy when, because of other activities, I was unable to be at Borley.

It was soon obvious that the task of reaching undisturbed ground below the cellar floor was not going to be an easy matter. Apart from the tons of earth and rubble that had been dumped to fill the whole cellar area, there was a tangle of scrap iron that included parts of a lorry, several twisted steel hurdles, a discarded plough, some cast-iron stoves, empty oildrums and other metal debris. But the holes grew rapidly larger and, with the aid of a team of schoolboy helpers and a length of heavy chain, most of the worst obstacles were eventually dragged clear. Many fragments of bone were found, all originating from domestic and farm animals, plus red deer. The first day's efforts ended, in a depressing drizzle, at dark.

Work was restarted at eight the following morning, Sunday. A steady stream of Press and other visitors arrived, all eager to peer into the holes and question me about what I was trying to discover. Some were also anxious to advance their own theories, recommending all manner of methods including explosives and metal detectors. I wondered how the people of Borley would respond to a few bangs in addition to the other disturbances.

Finally, because of the need to reduce the amount of time taken up in answering spectators' questions, I issued a press statement saying that the digging had four main aims: to look for any further human remains associated with the fragments discovered in 1943; to test the theory that a tunnel connected the rectory with the church; to seek the missing church plate and to explore the rumour that the rectory ground had been the site of mass burials during an outbreak of plague. Although this was not a full revelation of my objectives, it succeeded in lessening the interruptions.

On Sunday afternoon, with the permission of the owner, Mr R.T.B. Payne, we opened a small hole in the yard at Borley Place, next door to the church. There was some excitement when, a couple of feet down, we found the top of some curving brickwork. Removal of a large stone slab showed that we had broken into a covered well.

With the start, next day, of the working week, the number of visitors dropped. But so did aid from my helpers. From Monday to Thursday the digging was continued by Sandford and Richardson, with Sewell and one or two others putting in such time as they could.

It was comical to observe some reactions from Sandford. Richardson had a lengthy journey from his home and had made it clear that he would be able to put in only normal working hours. But Sandford, a wiry little man, lived much closer. His facial expression and wagging head when I first briefed him on what I wanted done made it clear that he doubted my mental stability. But when, with a view to speeding the work forward, I asked if he would stay on in the evening, earning overtime and working by the light of hurricane lamps, his refusal was instantaneous. It became noticeable that he always departed before dark.

On the Monday, by pre-arrangement, we were visited by my friend Kenneth Allsop, who was then a writer on the staff of the national weekly magazine *Picture Post.* He was accompanied by a colleague, the well-known photographer Thurston Hopkins. Although crippled by a wartime leg injury, the handsome Allsop was a tenacious journalist whose talents later took him to the forefront of his profession, bringing him particular distinction on television. His death, at the height of his attainments, was widely mourned.

Picture Post had sent the pair to cover my excavations and prepare a general review of the Borley case in the light of the anticipated SPR 'exposure' of Harry Price. I took them to meet, interview and photograph Ethel and Alfred Bull, the Coopers, the Hennings, the Williamses, the Bacons and others. The resulting feature appeared in *Picture Post* on 1 January 1955. A syndicated version was published in Australia's *Sydney Morning Herald.* Having posed a number of questions about Price's methods and mistakes, Allsop ended his article: 'It is unsatisfactory and it is puzzling and in some curious way that is in itself an extension of the strangeness of Borley. For it is like attacking a summer swarm of gnats: while busy swatting one, in the dim light more swirl into your vision, never quite tangible or within reach, but you know, later, that they were there by the bites.

We feel bitten by Borley.' Allsop's words were accompanied by a full-page reproduction of one of Hopkins' photographs. Headed 'Is this the Borley Rectory ghost?', it showed a view of the fenced-off and disused rectory gateway. Just beyond and below the wire-and-paling fence were three blurry shadows, one vaguely resembling a flying bird.

There was much excitement at *Picture Post* when the photograph was developed and printed. I was asked to go and give my opinion. Hopkins and the darkroom staff assured me that nothing had been done to create the mystery. Always suspicious of strange effects on photographs, I told them I was not persuaded that the shot showed anything abnormal. It was years later, after two similar experiences, that I found what I believe to be the explanation.

I was present when Hopkins took his picture, shooting from ground level so as to outline the gatepost and fence against the sky. He used a Rolleiflex camera, which has a twin-lens reflex arrangement, an upper optic conveying an image to the large viewfinder, while a lower lens captures the photograph. In certain close-up situations, the tiny discrepancy between the scenes captured by the upper and lower lenses can be significant. I believe the Hopkins shot was an example. In the shady light conditions prevailing in the lane, it was necessary to make a fairly lengthy exposure. The combination of this with the gusty breeze blowing at the time would have caused nearby undergrowth, moving in the wind, to appear as blurs on the photograph. The disused gateway was full of tall weeds.

A second picture taken on the same spot a few days later by another *Picture Post* photographer, Alex Dellow, and reproduced with the Allsop article, showed no sign of abnormality. But during the interval between the photographs the weeds in the gateway had been cut down.

It must be added that Thurston Hopkins never accepted my theory. In an exchange of letters in 1976 – almost twenty-two years after he had taken the picture – he told me that he was aware of the marginal difference, in twin lens reflex cameras, between what one sees and what one takes, but maintained that, at the distance he was from the gatepost, this could not have accounted for the oddity. He added: 'You say the weeds had been cut down before Dellow's visit. But again I say I do not think the dark mass could have been produced by weeds. It simply doesn't resemble plant life, and is clearly much further back in the picture plane. It would have needed a thick bush to produce that result.'

My 1954 digging at Borley went on until late October when, because of the deteriorating weather, I called a halt. I paid off the labourers and expressed suitable thanks to my volunteer helpers and my hosts, the Hennings, with whom I had stayed at Liston Rectory. (Sadly, it turned out that Alfred Henning was to live for only a further three months.) We had reached the original cellar floor in one or two places, the 'cold spot' hole getting down some two feet into previously undisturbed ground. All the holes were covered with sheets of corrugated iron and a barbed wire fence erected around the site.

Although I visited Borley several times during the winter and following spring, wet weather and my other engagements prevented a full resumption of digging until July. I was again aided by Sewell and Rayner, as well as a number of other volunteers. Some widespread publicity preceded and followed the reopening of operations, stories appearing in the London *Evening News, Evening Standard, Daily Telegraph, Sunday Graphic, Sunday Dispatch, Reynolds News, Manchester Daily Dispatch, Suffolk Free Press, East Anglian Daily Times, Psychic News, Two Worlds* and *Psychic Realm.* Eva Henning having moved away after the death of her husband, I was very kindly accommodated by friends of Ethel Bull, Mr and Mrs L. Crampton, at their home, Highfield Mill, Sudbury.

The *East Anglian Daily Times* story combined the news of my return with the information that the new rector of Borley-cum-Liston, the Reverend Edward Lanfrane Morgan Mathius, former vicar of St Philip's, Sydenham, London, was to be instituted on 28 July – the 'traditional day' for appearance of the Borley 'nun'. I heard that the bishop was 'not amused' by the paper's humorous headlines: 'Big day for Borley. Rector comes; "nun" expected.' This time the spectating visitors came in droves, a few of them proving a great nuisance in their inconsiderate invasion of private property. There were many sightseers from overseas.

On 10 July we made a discovery which finally confirmed the belief that the site had formerly been occupied by an older building. This was established by the finding of a section of wall constructed of two-inch bricks whose size, composition and mortaring clearly pre-dated the style of present-day bricks, which were standardized in 1625.

Continuing work produced the virtual clearance of parts of the extensive cellar area, and in places exploratory holes were sunk to depths well below the cellar floor. Some interesting items were found, including parts of the servant-summoning bells that were said to have been rung paranormally. Having got rid of most of the rubbish, progress was again slowed by the need for careful sifting of earth from formerly undisturbed areas. I saw that it was going to be a long job to carry out the total exploration I had in mind. Confining the digging to such times as I could get to Borley was obviously going to drag the business on for years. I discussed the problem with Sewell, who at once volunteered to act as my deputy and continue the project in my absence. The Bacons gave their agreement. I drove back to London feeling happy that work would proceed less sporadically and grateful for the aid of a reliable helper.

I returned to Borley on 28 July, attended the institution of the new rector – the forty-ninth at Borley since 1236 – and spent several after-dark hours chatting with the numerous visitors who stood about on the site hoping to catch a glimpse of the 'nun'. If she was there, no one saw her.

Later that summer I was contacted by Michael Peacock, the youthful and talented producer of the BBC's weekly current affairs television programme *Panorama*, which was then presented by Richard Dimbleby. I was invited to the Lime Grove television headquarters to discuss the possibility of *Panorama* covering the Borley story as updated by my categorization of the pre and post-Price witnesses and the digging. Sprawling in his chair, his feet on his desk, Peacock demonstrated an ability to conduct two or three telephone conversations and a face-to-face talk at the same time. But the pressure increased and his part in the conference was taken over by his assistant, Hugh Burnett, a tall, slim, kindly young man who was himself to achieve prominence as a television producer and humorous cartoonist.

Arrangements were made for a film unit to visit Borley. The job was done in two hard-working days, separated by a relaxing night at the Bull Hotel, Long Melford. Led by Burnett as location producer, the team consisted of Michael Henderson, a studious-looking interviewer/reporter, cameraman Terry Hunt and a sound recordist.

After filming an interview with me at the excavation site, I guided the unit on a tour similar to that provided for Allsop and Hopkins. I was, however, able to introduce an important additional witness – Dr Abernethy. There was also an interview (not at my suggestion) with Brigadier C.A.L. Brownlow, a well-known Spiritualist living nearby, who gave his opinion. The Coopers were filmed while seated in their garden. Terry Bacon was questioned in the churchyard. His grandfather, Henry Williams, who for personal reasons was unwilling to appear full-face (he said he had received unpleasant anonymous letters following publication of an account of his experiences) gave an 'over-the-shoulder' description of the oddities he had seen and heard.

Unfortunately, Ethel Bull was unable to keep a morning appointment with us. By the time we were able to return to her home, it was nearly dark. When I mentioned that there was no supply of electricity to Miss Bull's house, cameraman Hunt shook his head. 'No light, no film. Film costs sixpence a foot. It would be a sheer waste to try it like this.' Burnett was also despondent. 'We'll just have to leave it,' he said. 'We've got five witnesses anyway.'

But I was concerned beyond the immediate requirement. Here, I felt, was what might be the last opportunity to get this most vital witness on visible and audible record. We had arrived in a convoy of four cars. I suggested that they be arranged in a semicircle in the driveway, their headlights trained on the front door. This was done, and a test with a lightmeter proved satisfactory. Muffled in an overcoat, Ethel Bull sat with Michael Henderson on chairs in the centre of the blaze of light and told her story with clarity and humour.

At Burnett's invitation, I saw the 'rushes' at Lime Grove. Four days later, Hallowe'en, I was back in the studios for a 'live' interview with Richard Dimbleby as part of the telecast. The subject was handled with scrupulous fairness, Dimbleby being his usual courteous, though questing, self. Over drinks after the programme he told me that he took a keen personal interest in psychical research.

The filmed material came across effectively. Only Williams' contribution was omitted. Although Peacock added no firm conclusion as to the haunting, there was no tampering with witnesses' calm and unfaltering accounts. There were some favourable national press reviews, despite the pressure on space caused by Princess Margaret's announcement that she had decided to end her romantic involvement with Peter Townsend. The London *Evening Standard* asked Michael Henderson whether he believed in ghosts. 'I do now,' he said.

There was an amusing incident the day after the programme. In a Fleet Street tobacconist's I asked for a certain brand of cigarettes. Her jaw hanging open, the assistant handed me another make. When I pointed out the error, she apologized and added, 'It was just that you reminded me of a man who was on television last night, talking about ghosts. It gave me the creeps!'

Unhappily, the *Panorama* coverage did not provide everyone with satisfaction. Evidently under the impression that I was able to dictate to the producer what he should and should not include in his programme, Rayner wrote to me expressing surprise that 'no mention was made of the excavators who actually did the digging. After putting in so much digging time at Borley when the heat was intense and very tiring, it is my opinion and others that at least I should have been invited to Borley when the TV film was being made.' His letter ended: 'After taking into consideration previous incidents and this later one it is my intention not to do any more digging at Borley.'

I replied, pointing out that *Panorama* had allocated only fifteen minutes to the item, most of which had, rightly, been occupied by the statements of witnesses. I explained that the short notice given of the television proposal had allowed little time for essential arrangements, leaving no opportunity to invite the many interested people who might have wished to be present. Adding that I had no idea of the meaning of his reference to 'previous incidents', I assured him that, in respect of thanks to my helpers, it had always been my intention to deliver full acknowledgements when my own account of the Borley work was written.

Rayner neither acknowledged my letter nor abstained from further digging at Borley. What complex human reactions are aroused when the great god Publicity stalks the scene!

Another unhappy incident followed. My wife had sometimes accompanied me to Borley and had struck up an acquaintance with Betty Bacon and her children, spending time with them while I was engaged with the digging. One afternoon, as we were driving to the hotel in which we were staying, she surprised me by saying that she wished to return to Borley that evening as she had promised to give a seance in the cottage. For some months she had been attending a 'mediumship development circle' at Eva Rayner's *Temple*. Recalling Eva's comments to me about the degree of ability she had shown at those meetings (to spare her feelings I had not told her of Eva's remarks), I asked her not to proceed with the arrangement. She refused the request. By the time we reached the hotel, the matter had become a quarrel. When I asked what she would do if I refused to drive her back to Borley (she had no driving licence of her own), she answered that she would get a taxi. Against my will, we returned to the rectory cottage after dinner.

Betty Bacon had prepared a table and chairs for the 'seance'. The group consisted of her and her husband, Sewell, Williams, my wife and myself. The lights were lowered and the business began. Slumping in her chair, my wife appeared to go into trance. Her mouth barely moving, she repeated again and again: 'Very difficult. Go away. Leave us alone. No investigations.' That was all there was to it. After half an hour everyone was bored. The 'seance' broke up, and Betty served coffee. Trying to keep the peace, I avoided any mention of the episode in subsequent conversations with my wife.

A few months later the Spiritualist weekly *Psychic News* published an article written by A.D. Cornell, described as 'research officer of the Cambridge Psychical Research Society'. Headed 'The lesson of Borley: It is time for researchers and Spiritualists to co-operate', the piece contained some frothy observations. One paragraph read: 'I understand that some seances held in the old coach house have produced a certain amount of highly melodramatic trance-styled acting upon the part of a well-known recent investigator's wife – other than that "Marie Laire" [the supposed 'nun'] has not put in an appearance lately.' It was obvious that the 'well-known recent investigator' referred to could only be me. The description 'highly melodramatic trance-styled acting' clearly implied that my wife had attempted deliberate fraudulence. I received telephone calls from sympathizers, most of them expressing surprise at the news that my wife was a medium.

Incensed by the cheap slur, I consulted my solicitor. He said that, as my wife and I were readily identifiable from the article, Cornell's remark was defamatory. But as he had not been present at the 'seance', from whom had he gained the wounding description of my wife's performance? Cornell and Betty Bacon were asked to provide explanations. Betty replied with alacrity that she had not made the comment – and added that she had a witness to prove it!

Correspondence dragged on. After sending several evasive communications, Cornell addressed a rambling, repetitious letter to my solicitor offering an assurance that, although several people had expressed doubts about the genuineness of my wife's trance, 'no one ... was in any way trying to be malicious, contemptuous or unfair ... At no time was it suggested that Mrs Paul had been guilty of any deliberate fraud. [How 'melodramatic trance style acting' at a seance could be anything else was not explained!] ... Since making this report I now find that some of the people from whom I obtained information were not as experienced in psychical matters as they claimed to be. ... '

Weary of all the nonsense, I told my lawyer to leave it at that.

The 1955 excavations ended in mid-November. The holes were again roofed over with corrugated iron and the protective fence repaired and restored.

Having bought a planchette, Sewell spent many evenings at Borley during the winter, experimenting with seances in the rectory cottage. Although several members of her family participated from time to time, Betty Bacon was his most frequent co-operator. Among the yards of squiggles they produced, a number of 'communicators' inscribed meaningless messages on rolls of wallpaper. There were even some statements signed 'Harry Price', promising that persistence with digging would locate further human bones associated with the remains found in 1943. One message forecast a fatal shooting in a Cambridge bicycle shop on a specific date. All this 'information' proved wrong.

It seemed that Price's spirit was kept busy around that time. A week after publication of Dingwall, Goldney and Hall's *The Haunting of Borley Rectory* in February 1956, Spiritualist editor Maurice Barbanell ran a front-page article in *Two Worlds* headed 'Spirit message from Harry Price. "Borley is haunted ... it will prove itself ... I will be vindicated." ' Written by Barbanell, the piece revealed that he had received the statements attributed to Price during a sitting with a well-known clairvoyant, Lilian Bailey. 'Harry Price gave me a spirit message last week on the day that the book was published accusing him of faking some phenomena at Borley. He refuted the charge,' the article began.

' "The rectory is definitely haunted," he said. "Borley will prove itself and I will be vindicated, even if I have to go there and manifest myself." Though he admitted that much of the criticism in the book written by his two ex-colleagues [There were, of course, three authors, but Trevor Hall was even less of an 'ex-colleague' of Price's than the other two] was true, he refuted the accusation that he had done anything fraudulent. But he was adamant about the genuineness of the Borley hauntings.'

Pointing out that the SPR authors had alleged that many of the Borley phenomena happened only when Price was there, Barbanell reported that Mrs Bailey's spirit guide had told him that Price possessed 'latent physical mediumship'.

> Thus phenomena were more likely to happen in his presence. This is

> borne out by his secretary, Lucie Kaye, now Mrs Meeker, who repeatedly said that Price attracted poltergeist disturbances ...
>
> Another comment made by Price was that he was very interested in Philip Paul in his labours at Borley since his passing. If Price is now going to haunt Borley to prove that it was haunted when he was on earth, then fate will have produced a situation more paradoxical than any fiction writer could have dreamed. And some might say that it would be poetic justice if Price were to haunt the authors of the book which attacks him!

The spring and early summer of 1956 were persistently wet, creating conditions quite unsuitable for further exploration of the water-logged holes. I made several calls at the site and Sewell did some minor digging and tidying up. Then, in one of his letters, Sewell told me: 'We have definitely got to excavate and fill in all holes this year.' I answered that, although the Borley people had not mentioned this requirement to me, I assumed it had some connection with a plan to build a bungalow on the site – my wife having mentioned that Betty Bacon had told her of the scheme. When a local newspaper printed a statement about the intended building, Betty expressed annoyance, virtually denying the report. In a later letter Sewell withdrew his earlier message, commenting: 'As far as I know, they are quite willing for the digging to continue indefinitely, but it must be left safe and tidy for the winter.' Some odd new human undercurrents were obviously permeating Borley's already complex atmosphere.

I arranged a final burst of excavatory work in August that year, combining my daytime labours with some nights at the Half Moon Hotel, Clare, where there had been reports of unaccountable happenings. Although my days were busy, my slumbers were undisturbed. At Borley, much was accomplished in a short time. The weather held fine, and a good number of helpers put willing backs into the final effort. To add a finishing touch, Gordon Hick, sales director of Whitlock Brothers, a firm of agricultural and industrial engineers at Great Yeldham, Essex, provided, free of charge, a 'Dinkum Digger' Fordson Major mechanical excavator. Worked by an expert operator, the machine was used, with few pauses, for three days, removing virtually all the remaining filling from the cellar area and going well down into undisturbed ground. Its delicate handling capabilities enabled each scoopful of earth to be carefully examined, but nothing dramatic was found. Among the renewed press interest, I was interviewed by George Ffitch of Independent Television.

Convinced at last that there was nothing to be gained by prolonging the digging, still mindful of the Rayner and Cornell unpleasantness and facing the impossibility of constant attendance at Borley because of many other commitments, I announced the end of my excavations in the second week of August.

Betty Bacon's rejection of my offer to arrange and pay for restoration of the site was explained a week or so later, when reports reached me that Sewell, now again joined by Rayner, was continuing to dig. The bungalow plan had seemingly evaporated! But nothing was found by my erstwhile aides. This confirmed the outcome of a light-hearted experiment I had conducted earlier in the year when, asking ten leading mediums whether there was any subterranean discovery to be made at Borley, I received a unanimous 'no'.

Having spent uncountable hours and considerable money on the case, I was saddened to learn, later, of a slanted and deficient account of part of my work at Borley. By whatever means the incomplete and inaccurate information was gathered, the process included no approach to me. The reason for this omission, was, understandably, not disclosed.

There was a new twitch of excitement in the autumn of 1957, when contractors laying water pipes broke into an arched channel running under the lane between the rectory site and the church. A surveyor said it was a land drain. Drainage engineers whose opinions I sought laughed at a claim that it was a tunnel. 'In the days when "secret" tunnels were made, labour and materials were cheap,' said one. 'Tunnels were, therefore, constructed so that people could pass through them with reasonable ease and speed.' At its largest points, the Borley 'tunnel' measured thirty-two inches wide by twenty-eight inches high. Perhaps roomy enough for waterborne ghosts?

Acknowledgements

I acknowledge, with grateful thanks, the assistance I received from many voluntary helpers, of both sexes and a range of ages, during the digging at Borley. The excellent work they did, often under difficult conditions, was of great value. Apart from those already mentioned, the following were particularly helpful:

John Billet, of London
Cyril Botwright, of Ipswich
A.J. Brown, of Middlesex
R.J. Gaines, of Middlesex
S. Kiernander, of Worthing
Miss B.M. Knott, of Ipswich

Rev. John Dening, of Liverpool
R.J. Eaglen, of Cambridge
Patrick Emptage, of London
Gerald F. Lambert, of Bury St Edmunds
John O'Connell, of London
J.D. Willis, of Sudbury

6. Alarm at Abbas

I found the reputedly fourteenth-century Abbas Hall at the end of a long, unsurfaced track winding between overgrown hedges whose brambles all but blocked the way. Standing near Great Cornard, Suffolk, it was just a few miles from Borley. Neglected but in process of restoration, the small house consisted of ground- and first-floor rooms laid out in the shape of a reversed 'L'. There was no electricity supply or telephone. Distant from the nearest public road, it slumbered in an almost uncanny silence.

I had been asked to investigate 'eerie happenings' and was welcomed by the occupier, a slim, attractive young woman named Yvonne Spalding. We talked in the kitchen while she prepared lunch.

She told me she was divorced and devoted her time to her herd of pedigree Jersey cattle. The animals were looked after on the nearby estate of Lord Abinger, who, she said, was a personal friend. She occupied the house, which was sparsely furnished, rent free in exchange for keeping it in order. The owner was a young solicitor who had, it seemed, a taste for throwing parties and arriving unexpectedly. She thought he really wished her to leave so that he could let the place to Americans.

Over lunch she told me of inexplicable footsteps and 'heavy dragging noises' she and two others had heard moving across the floors of the two bedrooms which, with a bathroom, were the only usable parts of the upper floor. Instant searches had revealed no explanation of the sounds.

On another occasion, she said, when Lord Abinger had been alone in one of the two ground-floor living-rooms while she was preparing food in the kitchen, he had suddenly called out that an old woman was looking in through one of the windows. They had both rushed outside but found no one.

And then, one evening, when she had been alone, reading under an oil lamp beside the large fireplace in the main living-room, there had all at once been a loud 'click' from the latch of the door to the kitchen. Looking up, she had seen that her two pets, a dachshund bitch and a female Siamese cat, were both staring at the door. While she watched, their heads swivelled in unison as though they were observing someone, or something, moving across to another door that opened to the stairway. When the animals' eyes were directed towards the second door, that latch had also clicked. Neither door had opened and she seen nothing. But a few seconds later she had heard dragging footsteps passing across the floor of her bedroom immediately above. Terrified, she had scooped up the dog and cat and gone to spend the night with a friend.

By this time we had finished lunch and were relaxing when I heard two loud metallic clicks from the kitchen. The dachshund, dozing on my lap, the Siamese, in a box with some kittens, and another cat, sleeping on the sofa, paid no heed. Dropping the dog, I dashed into the kitchen but found nothing to account for the noises. We resumed our talk. Yvonne showed a strong curiosity about occultism, posing many unanswerable questions on such subjects as reincarnation and karma.

At five o'clock I drove her into Sudbury, where she wished to do some shopping. From there we went to Borley, where I introduced her to the Bacons and Mr and Mrs Williams. We also called at Liston Rectory for a talk with Alfred and Eva Henning, who were much taken by Yvonne's account of her strange experiences. When we left, it was growing dark.

I invited her to dinner at the Bull in Long Melford, but she said she was expecting people at Abbas, so we returned there. The owner, Cecil Wells, arrived with a young lady named Margaret Bird. They soon departed to dine in Sudbury, saying they would come back later. For the next hour or two I busied myself with a torch, making a close examination of each of the rooms and taking a number of flashlight photographs. Yvonne served a light supper.

Cecil and Margaret returned, bringing with them three friends: Ford, a doctor specializing in chest diseases, Peter, a local artist, and another young woman. Cecil produced a crate of beer and, grouped around the crackling log fire, we drank and chatted. When Yvonne suggested that we might have a 'seance' with a makeshift ouija board, Cecil said he would neither take part nor permit it in the house. Seeing that my interest was aroused by his vehemence, he said that an earlier ouija board session at Abbas had been followed by a car smash involving some of his guests. He believed that the 'seance' had in some way contributed to the accident. His emphatic ruling seemed to stifle the group. He and Ford left soon after midnight.

Yvonne again suggested the ouija. No one else expressing objection, a low, polished wooden table was brought down from a bedroom and Yvonne chalked the alphabet and the words 'yes' and 'no' in a circle on its surface. The lamps were turned down and everyone placed an index finger on an inverted wineglass in the centre of the table. There was instant movement but for some time the glass spelled out only incomprehensible rubbish. Gradually, in answer to spoken questions, understandable responses began. Typically, however, there was much contradiction and gibberish. My companions were excited by a message purporting to come from a man who claimed to have died five hundred years earlier. He promised to manifest himself in my bedroom that night. Having witnessed many ouija board promises, I did not allow it to raise my expectations.

We continued until the 'messages' again became nonsense. We stopped at 2.30 a.m. Peter departed with his young lady, and Yvonne, Margaret and I retired, the females occupying Yvonne's bedroom while I slept in a room on the other side of the staircase. The 'ouija entity' did not keep his promise; I spent an undisturbed night.

Persisting with my inquiries into the case, I decided to arrange a physical seance in the house, to see what such a test would produce. Having obtained Cecil Wells' permission, the medium I approached was John Scammell, a young man who sometimes gave sittings at Eva Rayner's *Temple*.

Because it was the easiest part of the premises to put under control, I chose Yvonne's bedroom for the experiment. Having blocked the chimney, I sealed the windows and blacked them out with thick blankets. The divan bed was moved against the wall, and chairs brought up from the ground-floor rooms were placed in a circle. Scammell having said he was prepared to work without a 'cabinet' (a curtained-off cubicle normally occupied by the medium and said to be necessary to 'concentrate the power') no such facility was provided. I was assisted with the arrangements by my wife, Yvonne and Alan Dick, a well-known *Daily Herald* reporter and one of the journalists who had accepted my invitation to witness whatever might result. We were later joined by Hugh McLeave, of the *News Chronicle*, John Rydon, of the *Daily Graphic*, who was accompanied by a young male cousin, and a reporter representing the *East Anglian Daily Times* and *Ipswich Evening Star*, who brought a female friend. Scammell arrived accompanied by a young woman, Marie Arnold, and two doctors named Cuming and Wilson. The party also included the former Eva Rayner and her *Temple* secretary, Stuart Laing, who had married seventeen months earlier. The small bedroom was filled to capacity.

For the benefit of those new to such proceedings, Cuming gave a brief explanation of physical mediumship. Scammell occupied a chair in a corner with Eva on one side of him and Cuming on the other. I sat against the only door, where I had control of an oil lamp and an electric torch. Rydon was on my right, McLeave on my left. My wife, Madge, occupied the chair next to Rydon, while Yvonne took the place beside McLeave. Alan Dick had, unfortunately, had to leave, but every seat was taken.

In the absence of a record-player, Yvonne produced a musical box. A single, luminous-banded aluminium megaphone – known to Spiritualists as a 'trumpet' – was placed in the centre of the circle. After locking the door and before extinguishing the lamp, I took a reading from a thermometer I had placed on the wall behind me. At the start of the seance, at 8.15, it registered 58° Fahrenheit. We plunged into total darkness.

After some introductory remarks by Scammell, hands were linked and Eva said a prayer 'for guidance and protection'. A few seconds later the trumpet was flung violently out of the circle and fell to the floor behind me, against the door. The musical box was turned off and some of the sitters began singing '*Ave Maria*', Marie's voice predominating. Very strong icy breezes were felt, producing nervous comments from some of the inexperienced.

Three times I heard the sound of low gurgling from Scammell's corner but on each occasion this was followed by his voice, saying he did not wish to lose consciousness. Finally, he began to give clairvoyance, which I noted as best I could in the blackness, using shorthand on a pad on my lap. The following is an extract:

> This building stands on the site of an early Dominican monastery, but there was a controversy about it and a heated battle was fought around here. The monastery was built elsewhere nearby. [The footings of an ecclesiastical building were said to be located in the grounds]. This building was used by refugees from the Great Plague in London. Then some Dutch people lived here. They had one child, a mentally deficient

> girl. She died by falling from an upper window of the house. Her father was accused of her murder and put into stocks not far from here. He disposed of her body in the well. [Abbas had two wells. Bones were said to have been recovered during work in the deeper one a short while earlier. These were reported to have been thrown with other refuse into a pond at the back of the house]. She is coming into this room now, through the door and into the centre of the circle. She wants to be seen. She has two teeth missing from her upper set.

The medium then requested knocks from the entity he had described. At once faint but distinct taps were audible, apparently occurring under the divan bed.

After other, minor, phenomena the seance ended at 9.30 p.m. Having relit the lamp, I checked the thermometer. It showed 52° – a drop of 6° from the reading of an hour and a quarter earlier, despite the presence of fourteen people in the small, tightly sealed room.

Changing their minds about their earlier announced intention of remaining overnight, Rydon and McLeave left with the other sitters. Yvonne also departed, to go to her parents' home in Chelmsford. By 10.30 Madge and I were alone. Soon afterwards there were knocks at the door, made not by spirits but by two twenty-one-year-old American airmen from the nearby Lakenheath base. Giving their names as Harvey McDowell and Elroy Gunther, they asked if they might 'look over the haunted house'. Evidently intrigued by the old building, they asked permission to stay the night. They helped with redistributing the furniture and brought in more logs for the living-room fire.

We talked until after midnight when, no doubt from a combination of fatigue and the effect of the drinks dispensed by the Americans, I fell asleep. I was prodded into wakefulness by Madge, who said she had heard footsteps crossing the floor of the 'seance room' bedroom immediately above. McDowell said he had also heard them, but Gunther had not. We searched the house but found no explanation.

Ashamed at my lack of alertness because of my imbibing, I was reminded of a story told me by an engaging veteran of the psychic scene named Evan Powell who, after starting his working life in a South Wales coalmine at the age of twelve, became a 'direct voice' medium. Through his friendship with the crusading Spiritualist and 'Pope of Fleet Street' journalist Hannen Swaffer, Evan was invited to give a seance for *Daily Express* proprietor Lord Beaverbrook. The Beaver insisted on prefacing the sitting with lavish liquid refreshment. As Evan had warned they might, the spirits consumed before the seance had a depressing effect on the phenomena he was able to produce. Disappointed, Beaverbrook commented: 'Not many spirits, were there?' 'No, my lord,' said Powell, 'they don't mix.' 'What don't mix?' demanded the Beaver. 'The disembodied and the disembottled,' said Evan.

Madge and I spent the remainder of the night in the seance room bedroom. Apart from an attack of toothache, I rested undisturbed. The Americans slept on the sofa and armchairs beside the fire downstairs. Next day – a Sunday – we rose early and finished tidying the rooms. We left in torrential rain and I drove the Americans to Sudbury, where they intended to catch a train back to their base.

During the afternoon Alan Dick telephoned and asked for details of the seance happenings. His story appeared in the *Daily Herald* the following day. The *East Anglian Daily Times* story also described the occasion:

> ... there were some shocks. A trumpet – the sort used at most seances – suddenly took flight and landed outside the circle. Was this the gesture of an angry ghost "outraged by frivolities"? With a suddenness which sent my pulse rate up the medium said "She is coming through the door now." Only the mediums saw her but everyone present (including journalists) agreed about this: there was a faint, very faint, slippered pattering on the floor. Most people felt icy little draughts moving about the room. I felt these, and duly bore in mind the draughtiness of the house. But the draughts were – well, not quite draughts, and the pattering not quite human pattering. How could anyone have thrown the trumpet from the circle with such force and not be caught in the act? I must confess to bewilderment.

As often happens, publicity brought swarms of sightseers. Calling Abbas Hall 'Britain's most haunted house', a London evening newspaper printed a statement that hundreds were converging on Great Cornard in search of the building and, finding themselves lost, were knocking up indignant villagers to ask the way.

It was impossible to continue investigating in the midst of this invasion. Having made arrangements to be kept informed of any new developments, I filed my records and awaited further events.

7. Mystery at St Magnus

Ghosts are not exclusively country-dwellers.

Standing cheek-by-jowl with London Bridge and the monument marking the outbreak of the Great Fire of 1666, the Wren church of St Magnus the Martyr occupies a site that is believed to have accommodated religious edifices for more than a millennium. Damaged during the German air raids of 1940, the church was closed for eleven years. During that time the then rector, the Reverend H.J. Fynes-Clinton, conducted his services in the crypt.

Shortly before the war, Fynes-Clinton received three independent reports of sightings of a cowled spectre in the church and vestry. The witnesses were the wife of a former rector, a verger and a middle-aged female parishioner. After carefully noting their accounts of their experiences and questioning them closely on details, Fynes-Clinton informed Harry Price. Busy with other activities, Price was unable to find time to devote much attention to the case. I decided to look into it.

I visited Fynes-Clinton at his home in Westminster's St Ermin's Hotel in 1951. Well-built, sharp-eyed and keen-eared, he possessed an alert mind and clear memory that disavowed his octogenarian years. He told me he had been inducted at St Magnus in 1921.

He recounted the stories of the monk-like phantom seen at the church. The first sighting, by the former rector's wife, a Mrs Gallagher, had occurred in the main building. The figure, silent and unmoving, had appeared to be wearing a brown habit and was in a kneeling posture beneath a picture of Christ near the tabernacle. Apparently viewing it in profile, Mrs Gallagher was unable to see the face because of an obliterating shape like a raised hood. Within a few seconds the apparition melted away.

The second sighting happened in the vestry. It was reported by a devoted worker at the church, a Miss Few, who knew nothing of Mrs Gallagher's experience. Afflicted by deafness, Miss Few had the compensations of good eyesight and manual dexterity that made her an expert needlewoman. She had become accustomed, when engrossed in this work, to suddenly finding people near her without hearing anything of their approach.

Sitting alone in the vestry and concentrating on an intricate piece of embroidery one afternoon, Miss Few had, after a while, noticed from the corner of her eye that someone was standing close by. Observing that the person was wearing a straight, cassock-like draping, she assumed that the rector had joined her in the room. For a few seconds she went on with her stitching. Then, without lifting her head, she darted another quick glance towards her silent companion. At once her knowledge of fabrics told her that the weave of the cassock was much coarser than anything worn by Fynes-Clinton. Her busy fingers stopped and she raised her head, her eyes travelling over the figure that stood just a few feet away. When her gaze reached the upper part of the form, she saw that the head was enclosed by a cowl made from the same material as the cassock. But the cowl, which was open towards her, was empty – there was no face inside it! Dropping her work, she fled to find Fynes-Clinton, who was in the church. He managed to calm her, and together they had returned to the vestry. The figure had gone.

The third witness, the verger, a former regular soldier named Ridley, who had not been told of the ladies' experiences, approached Fynes-Clinton in a condition of extreme agitation shortly after the conclusion of a service. Noting that the man was very pale and seemed to be in a state of shock, Fynes-Clinton asked him what was wrong. Begging the rector to believe that he was neither intoxicated nor of unsound mind, the old soldier told of seeing the figure of a monk standing gazing down at a tomb to the right of the altar. Before he had had time to move or cry out, the apparition had vanished.

The tomb referred to, Fynes-Clinton told me, was that of Miles Coverdale, a former rector of St Magnus's and a post reformation Bishop of Exeter. In 1535 Coverdale achieved distinction for the first full English translation of the Bible. On his death, in 1568, he had been buried elsewhere but was later reinterred at St Magnus's. His sepulchre, cemented in, was the only occupied vault left in the crypt, said Fynes-Clinton. All the other human remains had been cleared away thirty or forty years earlier.

Fynes-Clinton made no secret of the fact that he believed the monk-like phantom was the ghost of Miles Coverdale. Interested in psychical research, he welcomed my proposal of some mediumistic tests in the church. I asked whether he had himself experienced anything odd at St Magnus's. He said he had not, but went on to tell of a curious event, away from the church, that had stimulated his interest in studying the paranormal.

He explained that he had taken a leading part in forming a society whose objective was to encourage public awareness of the churches in the City of London. The organization was called Friends of the City Churches. One day, while addressing an open-air meeting in furtherance of the society's aims, he had seen a parishioner named Newman join his audience. Remembering that the man had been seriously ill, he was surprised to see him at the meeting. As soon as the event ended, he went to the place where Newman had been standing but found that he had gone. The following day, he learned that Newman had died forty-eight hours earlier.

St Magnus's was reopened for public worship on 1 June 1951. Impressively redecorated and refurbished, its panelling, paintings and other artefacts struck me as somewhat overpowering. A large highly coloured effigy of the saint, wearing a distinctly unsaintly expression and grasping a model of the church in its left hand and an immense battle-axe in its right, watched over part of the roomy interior. Formerly the Earl of Orkney, St Magnus was martyred in 1116.

Soon after entering the darkening building – it was nearing dusk – I became aware of a scuttling movement among the empty pews. This turned out to be a female cat, strangely called Michael, which had, I was told, taken up residence during the blitz. I reflected that I had heard of church mice – now I had met a church cat!

The walls of the vestry were hung with old prints and documents, including part of a handwritten insurance policy dated 1720 and issued to Sir Christopher Wren by the Sun Insurance Company. Proudly, Fynes-Clinton drew my attention to a fine set of Chippendale chairs he had assembled in the room. In the courtyard behind the church, he showed me some ancient timbers which he said were parts of some of the piling from the original London Bridge. I commented on the evident antiquity of the flagstones covering the area. He replied that, when some of the stones had been lifted some time earlier, many human bones had been found just below the surface. He thought that the place had been used for speedy mass burials during the Great Plague of 1665 – the worst of several outbreaks of pestilence that afflicted London over the years.

I took Eva Rayner to St Magnus's – her first visit there and her first meeting with the rector – in July 1951. We sat in a pew at the rear of the church while she gave her clairvoyant impressions. Fynes-Clinton listened eagerly to her every word.

She began by saying that she felt him to be correct in his surmise about the identity of the ghost. She believed that the former incumbent wished his earthly remains to be removed from the church and was trying to indicate this desire by his sombre manifestations. After a pause, she spoke of 'a little lady who is very thin and bent. She died five or six years ago. She is tending the tapestries on the altar and is handling the lacework very lovingly.' Fynes-Clinton identified this description as that of a former worker at the church. One of her voluntary tasks, he told us, had been to look after the linen and she would have taken special care in maintaining the altar tapestries. She had been crippled in an accident, suffering injuries that had left her bent in a stoop.

Eva went on with various pieces of information that were personal to Fynes-Clinton, most of which he acknowledged as correct. Then she said: 'I have an impression of people lining up at the tabernacle as though they are awaiting blessings.' To this Fynes-Clinton commented: 'Standing beside the tabernacle is the figure of Our Lady of Walsingham, in Norfolk. In the old days pilgrimages went from here to the shrine at Walsingham, where they would line up for blessings.' Walsingham is reputed to have been the scene of 'miraculous' healings.

Eva said she was hearing the name 'Ellen' and was convinced it had belonged to a woman, now dead, who had attended St Magnus regularly and frequently wore a green coat. Fynes-Clinton said that Ellen was the name of a deceased relative of his who had been a worshipper at the church. She had often worn a bright green overcoat.

Afterwards, as we walked up the redolent Fish Street Hill towards the point where I had parked my car, Eva gave a sudden, immense shudder. As it was a warm evening I asked how she could possibly be feeling cold. 'I'm not cold,' she answered, and added, jerking her head back towards the church, 'It's something from there – a great, terrible, evil from the past.' She would say no more.

I was unable to return to St Magnus's until the following October. Then I arranged another test seance, this time setting a more difficult task for a sensitive experienced in 'automatic writing', Daphne Lloyd-Evans.

As with the ouija board, an early version of which is said to have been used for seances by Pythagoras and his followers, the origins of the 'automatic' production of script are buried in the mists of time. Some mediums are said to go into total trance for the process, while others remain conscious and apparently watch what they are writing. Most say that their hands are controlled and guided, and the messages written, by personalities other than their own. Dr Charles Richet, the eminent French physiologist, recorded experiments with a psychic who had no knowledge of Greek but who, during an automatic writing seance, produced several pages written without error in that language. One of the best-known British exponents, Geraldine Cummins, told me she received words clairaudiently and put them on paper in the normal manner. She said her writings, which never required revision, had once been timed at 1,750 words per hour.

Mrs Lloyd-Evans was assisted by her husband David, a hypnotist. With his aid, she usually fell into a light trance, her eyes closed and her head slumped on his shoulder. Her automatism was confined to her hand from the wrist, making it necessary for David to move the paper so that her writings appeared in lines instead of on top of each other.

Accompanied by a Press photographer friend, Gordon Banks, I drove to the Lloyd-Evans' home in Hampstead. Given no information about our destination, they occupied the rear seats of the car. We travelled, via Camden Town, Russell Square, Holborn and Fleet Street, to Cannon Street, where I stopped. David and Daphne were then securely blindfolded with heavy scarves. I completed the journey by a circuitous route through side streets, to reduce any sense of our direction.

Retaining his blindfold, David was guided into the vestry by Fynes-Clinton. I followed, steering Daphne. The blindfolds were then removed and introductions made. Since he was wearing the collar of his office and the room was easily identifiable as part of ecclesiastical precincts – a large crucifix was conspicuous among the furnishings – David and Daphne were then aware that they were in an old vestry.

When we were positioned round the table, a notepad was placed under Daphne's right hand and a pencil put into her fingers. David sat on her right. Within a few seconds her eyelids drooped and her head sagged to the right, going somewhat behind her husband. Frantic movements of the pencil started almost at once, sounding loud in the otherwise silent room. The following are extracts from the lengthy script produced, with Fynes-Clinton's subsequent comments.

Script: I am here with you. I am known as Elfreda. I have been here for a long while. It was my place when with you. I was so happy with you. It is my home.

Note by F-C: The church was a Saxon foundation before the conquest.

Question by F-C: Were you here before the Norman conquest?

S: Yes. Wait. I will go back. It is very long ago. Somewhere near 912.

N by F-C: The church was probably founded about 900 AD.

Q (PP): Can you tell us the name of this place now?

S: The church of the holy ... Mary. (F-C shook his head. David said 'No'.)

S: The church of the holy martyr.

Q (F-C): Can you tell us the name of the King at that time?

S: The King was Edward some of the time.

N by F-C: Yes. Edward the Confessor gave the church to Westminster Abbey.

Q (PP): How old were you when you left this place?

S: Twenty-three.

Q (PP): Were you a member of the church?

S: In a way, but I was more of a helper. I used to help at the great service.

N by F-C: Why not mention the Mass, which was the great service?

Q (PP): Do you spend only part of your time here or are you always here?

S: Part of me is here a lot but I do not always inhabit this place. I have a half here which keeps me attached, but it is not my only place.

N by F-C: Does this mean a burial? (A short pause followed)

S: I am Walter de Courcy.

Q (PP): Were you a worshipper here?

S: I was in charge of the choir and assisted in the general running of the church.

Q (PP): How long ago were you here?

S: I should say about seven hundred years.

N by F-C: I.e. about 1250.

Q (F-C): Did you take part in any special kind of service?

S: Sometimes the holy communion.

N by F-C: Why does he not call it Mass? Translated through a non-Catholic mind?
Q (F-C): Was this place connected with the river in any way?
S: This place was used as a refuge when I first knew it. It was filled with people escaping from the great pestilence. They came here to be safe.
Q (PP): Why would they be safe here?
S: Because they could be the other side.
Q (PP): Do you mean the other side of the river?
S: Yes. Water was to purify.
Q (PP): Was the pestilence worse on the other side then?
S: Yes. It was very dreadful. Those who came here were stricken with fear.
Q (PP): Were there any doctors here or was there any form of treatment?
S: No. It was for us to do what we could and give help and prayer. Some used herbs and potions but many died in spite of it.
Q(PP): Did the people cross the river by boat or bridge?
S: In boats or swam.
Q (PP): Was there no bridge then?
S: The bridge that is there now was not but there may have been another but they could not use bridge because water purified.
Q (PP): Were people not allowed to cross the bridge then?
S: No, because the pestilence had to be cleansed by water.

When, after about half an hour, Daphne showed signs of restiveness, the test was stopped. Fynes-Clinton remarked that the vestry had been built long after the church – in 1830 – and he wondered whether the comparatively modern environment might affect communications. He suggested another test, in the church itself. Daphne said she was willing, so we moved into pews to the right of the aisle. With David beside her she rested the notepad on cardboard on her lap.

More questions and answers followed, mostly about the bridge and the river. When Fynes-Clinton asked what trade had been carried on in the parish, the response came in the form of a crude drawing of a knife, accompanied by the explanation 'Used for cutting animals and fishes.' Fynes-Clinton's subsequent note on this read: 'Fishmongering has been the central trade of the parish since Roman times. A neighbouring parish also contained a large animal slaughterhouse;

this was probably once within the bounds of the parish of St Magnus.' Other information given was not so easily checkable and less conclusive. There was no mention of Coverdale.

Back in the vestry Fynes-Clinton told me of a strange incident which had occurred in the church the previous Friday. Preparing for Mass that morning, he had been standing near the door when he was surprised to see a black-clad figure moving through the church from the direction of the altar. The form's movements were accompanied by such footfalls as would be made by hard-soled shoes on stone. The shape went behind a pillar and did not reappear. Fynes-Clinton said he had assumed it was his verger, who was in the church at the time. But the verger had approached him after Mass and told him he too had heard unaccountable footsteps in the church before the ceremony. No explanation had been found and to the best of their knowledge there had been no one else in the church at the time.

David and Daphne Lloyd-Evans emigrated to New Zealand the following year.

8. Nightmare Home

Shaped by long experience of human imperfections, British police regulations cover virtually all the emergencies that beset mankind. *Virtually* all. Not *all*. The policeman's 'bible' includes no directions on how to handle a poltergeist.

Rarely can the well-ordered constabulary of South London have wished more profoundly for the detective genius of Sherlock Holmes than they did one summer. Their difficulty began during a dark night in July, the first-quarter moon obscured by heavy clouds. The seedy back streets of West Norwood rested in the deep stillness of the early hours, the silence broken only by the clanking of an occasional goods train through the deserted station.

All at once new and urgent sounds echoed along well-worn pavements. The noises of speeding feet and panting breath. Reaching his objective, a young man flung himself into a telephone kiosk, snatched up the receiver and dialled '999'. 'For God's sake help us,' implored the caller, twenty-six-year-old Cecil Greenfield. 'We're being driven out of our minds.' His home, he gasped, was in the grip of a horror which had forced his family out of their beds and into a terrified group huddled in the living-room. They could stand it no more; the police must come at once.

The officer put the usual questions. What exactly was the trouble? Were his family being attacked? Was someone loitering with intent to commit a felony? Or was it just a simple breach of the peace?

'No,' said Cecil, a little calmer. 'The rooms are empty. But every few minutes there are crashes and bangs, an awful moaning sound and weird lights that dart around in front of your eyes. Please come quickly; it's driving us mad.'

'Very well. I'll get someone along as soon as I can.' The cool voice made no attempt to disguise the belief that it was talking to a lunatic.

But the promise was kept. Within minutes, Police Inspector Sidney Candler travelled to the house – 5 Langmead Street – with the crew of a radio car. They were admitted by the still-shaking Cecil.

Sure enough, the inhabitants were crouched together in the living-room, day clothes thrown over their night attire. They were Cecil's father and mother, a frail-looking, bespectacled sixty-nine-year-old and a diminutive, silver-haired sixty-year-old, their second son, twenty-two-year-old Dennis, his twenty-year-old wife Gladys, Gladys' mother, in her fifties, her son Gordon, aged eight, and the Greenfields' daughter Patricia, aged fourteen.

The strange disturbance seemed to realize that the law had arrived. All was quiet. Led by eagle-eyed Candler, the policemen examined the house from loft to cellar. They found nothing out of the ordinary. But as soon as they made to leave, the Greenfields begged them to stay. Cups of tea were produced. Dawn began to light the rooftops. Daylight brought a strengthened atmosphere of serenity. Those of the family who did not have to go to work breathed more easily and snatched some sleep.

But the following night Cecil raced once more to the telephone box. It had all started up again.

This time Candler brought with him a squad of eight constables. It was a puzzle he was determined to unravel. The eight residents in the house were placed in the living-room, and a constable was posted outside its only door. The other officers were stationed at various points throughout the building. Candler took up a roving patrol. Now the mysterious presence was not deterred by the company of the police, despite their number. During their vigil, with the family secure in the living-room, there were raps, crashes and moans from the loft, the quilt was unaccountably snatched from a bed and a picture crashed from a wall, its cord unbroken and the hook undisturbed.

Inevitably, with the nocturnal comings and goings of policemen, the neighbours began to talk. Rumours spread. The first of a stream of newsmen descended on the house. They found the inspector perplexed but quotable. 'We have searched the premises and are baffled,' Candler told reporters. 'I was sceptical when I received the first report of the matter, but after interviewing the Greenfields I am convinced something strange is happening.'

The headlines spread from the local Press to the national dailies, to provincial papers and even overseas: 'Police Keep Midnight Vigil to Arrest a Ghost.' 'Ghost! So Police Stay With Family.' 'House Where Family Dare Not Go To Bed.'

I began my inquiries at Langmead Street on 18 July. The house, an ordinary working-class dwelling, contained six rooms arranged on three floors. Standing in a little L-shaped back street of only ten homes, at the rear of a factory producing office furniture, near West Norwood station, it had been requisitioned by the local council and re-roofed and repaired after wartime damage.

I began by interviewing the Greenfields individually and then as a group, checking carefully for any discrepancies or contradictions in what they told me. The family appeared to be genuinely terrified. During our conversations it was obvious that they were constantly on the alert for any resumption of the disturbances. The senior Mr and Mrs Greenfield and Cecil and Patricia said that, whenever possible, they had taken to leaving the house each evening to spend the night with friends. Having nowhere else to go, Dennis, Gladys, her mother and young Gordon remained at home but said they were often awakened by the unaccountable noises and had spent many nights huddled together on living-room chairs.

Cecil, Dennis and their mother claimed that they had begun to notice strange sounds soon after moving into the house four years earlier. The noises had seemed to come from the roof and loft, like a gentle tapping on the tiles. It was then audible only to people in the second-floor rooms. At first, birds or mice had been suspected, but there were none of the usual traces left by such visitors. Gradually, the taps had grown to thuds and the thuds to crashes that could be heard all over the house. These sounded like 'coal being broken and furniture dragged'. But there were no coals or furniture in the loft. The outbreaks had become more and more frequent during the preceding few weeks. Some of the sounds resembled footsteps. Dennis said these were 'like something walking on the ceiling'.

It had all come to a head, Cecil told me, during the early hours of 11 July. Half awake, he had heard a tiny sound suggestive of a person moving about just outside the door of his first-floor bedroom. He had thought someone was feeling unwell and making their way downstairs to get a drink of water or some medicine. But the sound ceased. Then it came again, still from just the other side of his door. Slipping out of bed, he had opened the door and stepped onto the landing. To his surprise, all was dark and deserted. Thinking someone might have descended to the kitchen, he had turned to go downstairs. Then, as his eyes became adjusted to the dimness, he had noticed a movement just below. Rounding a bend in the staircase and ascending towards him was a man-sized grey-white shape.

Horrified and rooted to the spot, he had gazed at the thing as it continued its upward way. No face was discernible but he had had an impression of arms folded at breast height across the figure. Slowly the phantom had advanced. As it came nearer, he had become aware of an icy coldness which gradually increased in intensity, 'with a sort of electric vibration'. When the approaching shape passed over a loose board on the stairway, there had been a creak as would have been made by a normal application of weight. The sound had seemed to release him from his helplessness, Cecil explained. He had screamed. Instantly, although it was almost within touching distance, the apparition had vanished. Roused by his cry, his mother and father had rushed from their bedroom on the same floor. They found Cecil, white and shaking, still scarcely able to move.

It seemed that, five days later, the faceless phantom had been seen again – this time by two witnesses. Arriving home at 2.15 a.m. after attending a party, Dennis and Gladys had quietly opened the front door and entered the hallway. Then, looking towards the staircase, they had seen a tall, grey-white figure standing some seven or eight steps up. Again, no face had been visible, but they had both seen outlines like arms hanging at the sides. Badly frightened, they had run to a neighbour's house. When they returned, accompanied by friends, the figure had gone.

There had, I was told, also been a daylight sighting of the form. Patricia had seen it, again on the stairs, one afternoon. A healthy, sports-minded girl, she had been severely shocked, for the first time in her life coming near to hysterics.

During my interviews, note-taking and detailed inspection of the building, a sizeable crowd had gathered outside. Many callers asked if they might come in 'to see the ghost'. The weary Greenfields asked me to deal with these requests. During that first visit, from 6.45 to 10.15 p.m., I dealt with inquiries from four members of a local psychical research society, two newspapermen, three individual part-time ghost-hunters and an uncounted number of curiosity-seekers.

One caller, who said he was a policeman from an Essex village, was particularly persistent with his offer of aid in my investigation. He was, he said, willing to remain in the house overnight. Impressed by his candid manner and because other commitments made it impossible for me to stay until the morning, I obtained the Greenfields' consent to his vigil.

His telephoned report next day said that he considered the strange effects to be entirely normal in origin. He felt sure, he told me, that all the 'phenomena' had arisen from natural causes, vibration from the nearby railway, wind and reflections from street lamps accounting for the knockings and 'ghosts'. I told him I found it difficult to accept such swift judgement on the basis of a single night's watch and asked whether he considered the occupants of the house to be mistaken rather than mischievous. He said he did, indicating that he had not detected any trickery. It later emerged that he had antagonized the Greenfields by his somewhat militaristic methods. They refused to allow him in the house again.

The question I put to my temporary aide is fundamental to the investigation of claims of paranormal experience. Some understanding of the possible motivation of the claimant is essential in assessing the probabilities of the case. For obvious reasons, claims of hauntings in public houses, theatres and hotels are suspect from the start. The presence of a 'ghost' in such establishments can be a significant stimulus to business. Nor is the private home automatically above suspicion. Alleged sufferers from domestic poltergeist infestations are sometimes over-imaginative publicity-lovers. They may have other motives. In one case I dealt with, a man was trying to frighten away his unwanted wife so that he could bring his mistress to live in the house. In another a wife was trying to scare a husband she suspected of being unfaithful. When council-owned dwellings are involved, a 'ghost' is sometimes a ruse aimed at persuading local authorities to provide better accommodation.

My suspicions were aroused by the knowledge that 5 Langmead Street was council-owned. I did not have long to wait to discover that I was not the only person entertaining that particular doubt. As I left the house after my first visit, a grubby boy detached himself from the crowd and tugged at my sleeve. 'Know wot I fink abaht it, guv?' he said. 'They've got a lot o' mice in their 'ouse an' they wants the cahncil ter give 'em a new plice. So they've decided ter 'ave a ghost 'cos they fink that'll git the cahncil ter move 'em aht inter somefink bet'er.' I thanked him for his opinion and bore it in mind. But it was not necessary to retain the idea for long. What I saw over the weeks that followed persuaded me that, far from gaining any advantage from their ghost, the Greenfields were being heavily punished by it.

This point of view was reinforced when I learned that the senior Mr Greenfield, himself a council employee, had, soon after the disturbance began, asked the housing office to find him and his family another home – and had been told outright that there was no possibility whatever of any alternative accommodation becoming available for some years. Confronted with this categorical rejection, one would have expected any manufactured 'ghost' to vanish as quickly as it had materialized. Instead, the disturbances had grown more intrusive.

Nor were these facts the totality of my reasoning. As the publicity spread, the Greenfields' lives became even more nightmarish. Their home was besieged by cranks and sensation-seekers. Crowds gathered outside as dusk fell each evening. Arriving by almost every form of transport, the unwanted spectators spent the hours of darkness gazing up at the windows and hammering at the door with requests to be allowed in. Cars and motorcycles arrived and departed throughout the night, jostling for parking space among the groups of people in the tiny street. Some of the visitors even chipped at the brickwork in their determination to carry away some souvenir. Several times the police had to be summoned to prevent sightseers gaining entry by force. Apart from the night-long noise of engines, the slamming of car doors and the racket of banter shouted among the onlookers, people also brought portable radios, ate and drank refreshments in their vehicles and threw their empty bottles and other litter into the road.

Sometimes, exhausted by lack of sleep and the unceasing stream of callers, some of the Greenfields went to stay with friends overnight. But as the disorders continued even this escape was cut off. Their hosts began to find excuses to avoid accommodating them. As the Greenfields soon realized, their helpers had become apprehensive that, with members of the afflicted family repeatedly entering their homes, the strange happenings might follow.

There was worse to come. Afraid of remaining in their house at night, the family became fearful of leaving it during the day. As soon as they were seen in the streets, they were pursued by catcalls and taunting advice that they should have their heads examined.

During my fourth call at Langmead Street, having parked my car some distance away and elbowed my way through the throng, I decided to put the Greenfields to a test which would, I considered, throw some light on the question of whether they were knowingly creating the mysteries. Pale and hollow-eyed, the family sat edgily on their usual chairs in the living-room. Just outside the window were the noises of engines, the chattering of the crowd, bursts of laughter, shrieks and the occasional thud of rubbish thrown at the door. As gently as I could, I said, 'Of course, if your ghost isn't real, you could stop all this discomfort very quickly. Simply give an interview

The author's father, mother, brother and sister

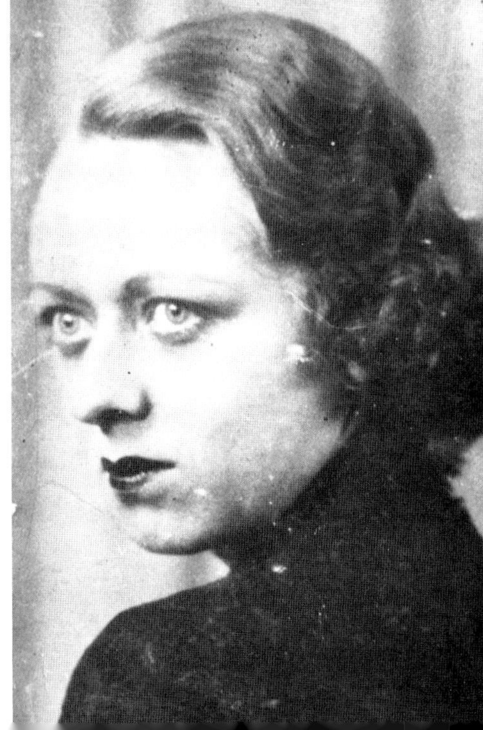

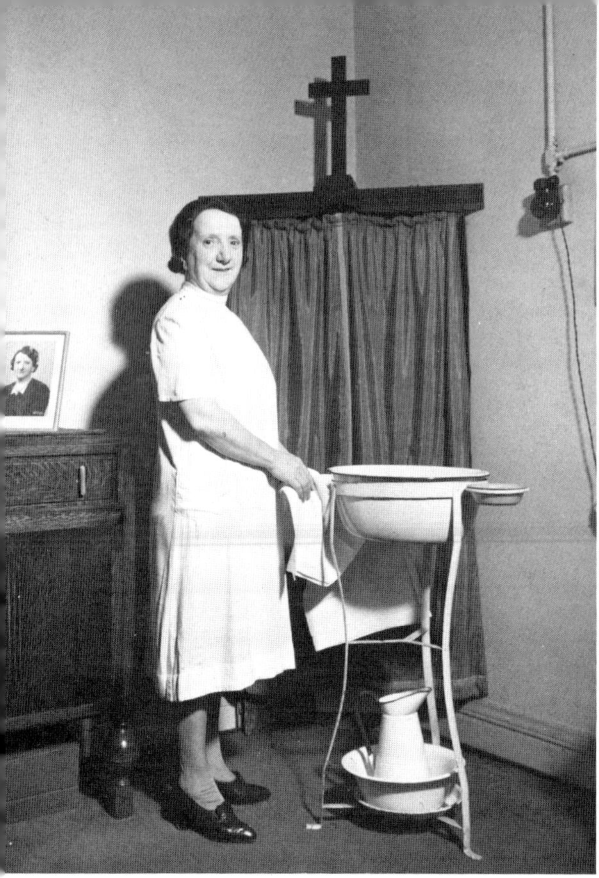

Medium/healer Eva Rayner in her Palmers Green centre in North London

The author in conversation with novelist/historian James Laver (right) and Isle of Man occultist Dr Gerald Gardner

The BBC TV *Panorama* team interviewing the author during his excavations on the site of Borley Rectory. Interviewer Michael Henderson holds the microphone; location producer Hugh Burnett looks on. Leonard Sewell holding spade. Cameraman Terry Hunt

Borley Rectory cottage, scene of extraordinary experiences, viewed from the top of Borley Church tower

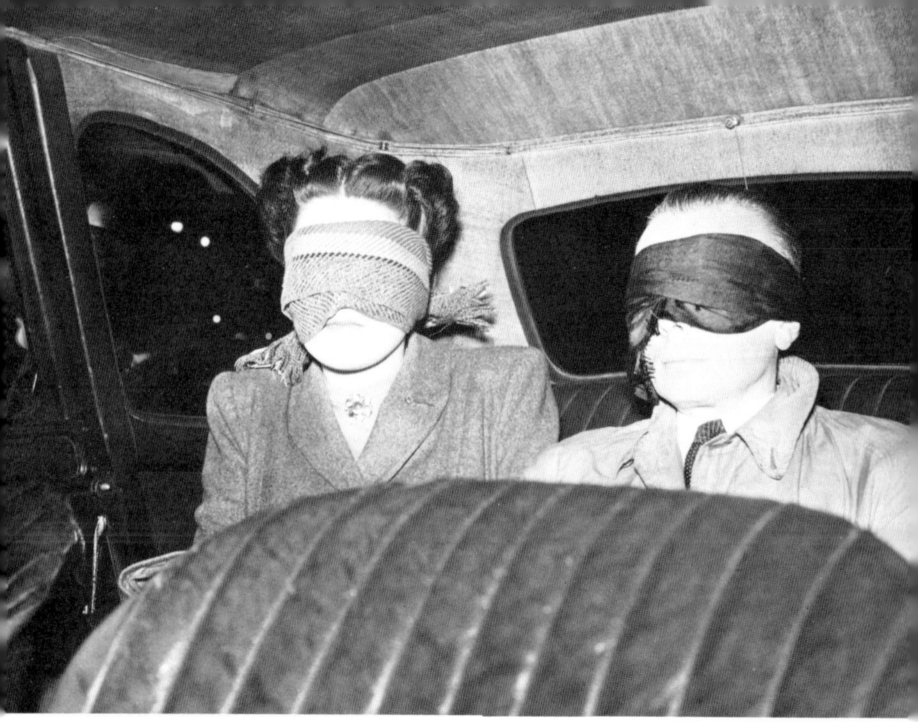

Above: Blindfolded in the author's car, David and Daphne Lloyd-Evans *en route* to the automatic writing experiment at St Magnus the Martyr church, near London Bridge

Left: The 'automatic writing' test in progress. The rector, th Rev H.J. Fynes-Clinton, looks on

Opposite: In the 'haunted' Camberwell Palace theatre, th author operates the heavy apparatus which was the only method of raising the curtain. Among other extraordinary events, the curtain was seen to rise of its own volition

Runcorn 'poltergeist boy' John Glynn in his wrecked bedroom

Blindfolded medium Ena Twigg psychometrizing the 'evil' painting, watched by its owner Mrs Dorothy Jenkins

"Do you really believe in Gilbert Harding?"

Friendship after their *What's My Line?* television encounter. Gilbert Harding with the author at *Picture Post's* 1953 Christmas party

The 'dead miner' photograph. Until the true explanation was found, it was believed to be a paranormal portrait of collier James Richards, taken after his burial in Treorchy, South Wales

The Amityville horror home, scene of six murders and world-publicized as the focal point of terrifying paranormal disturbances

to the press and say you invented it as a joke. Then you'll only have to suffer for a day or two longer, after which it will all die away and soon be forgotten.'

Their careworn expressions remained as listless as ever. Then Dennis spoke. 'These happenings and the crowds every night are turning us into nervous wrecks. But suppose we said we'd invented the ghost and the noises get worse or something else happens so we have to call the police in again? Nobody would believe us at all next time.' The others nodded agreement. I felt that my basic question had been answered. And the patient policemen were summoned several times more.

Sometimes the poltergeist seemed to know when the officers were about, often staying silent during their presence and then apparently greeting their departure with extra-vigorous demonstrations. Once, just after they had left at daybreak, the family heard heavy footsteps clumping downstairs from the deserted upper rooms. Fortified by the daylight, the Greenfields searched the house from roof to cellar. Everything seemed normal. But as soon as they were all back in the living-room, the thumps started again. Next, teacups in the kitchen were inexplicably moved. A spoon was heard rattling in a sugar basin in a closed cupboard. A large photograph fell from its frame, leaving the glass front and cardboard backing undisturbed. A shopping basket was hurled along the narrow hallway.

At times even the family's living-room sanctum was invaded. 'Brilliant luminous flashes' were seen by all the members of the household. The light was switched on and off without human agency. The senior Mr Greenfield suffered an unpleasant shock when the radio at his elbow started playing without anyone having switched it on. I checked all the switches in the house, and the controls of the radio. None was loose or faulty.

Dennis told me of a particularly alarming experience. Entering a bedroom one evening, he had seen Patricia's mattress 'lifting and curling up' as though manipulated by unseen hands. Patricia was then away from the house, having been sent for a short holiday with an aunt. Exerting all his strength, Dennis said, he had tried to push the mattress back into its normal place but, to his horror, found he was unable to make the slightest impression on it. Suspended in mid-air and defying both the laws of gravity and the young man's efforts to move it, the mattress had seemed to possess a will of its own. Suddenly, in the midst of this strange tussle, 'something' had seized Dennis from behind. He had swung round, only to see empty space. But his intangible attacker had maintained the grip for several seconds, tearing his shirt. He had ended up soaked with perspiration from his exertions. I examined the garment, which was almost new, and saw that it had been badly ripped around the buttons at the chest, as might happen in the case of seizure and pulling from the rear.

Various religious bodies visited the house. A band of worshippers from the Church of Nazarene knelt in prayer for removal of the ghost. A local Spiritualist group arranged a seance in the kitchen. The medium said that Dennis was the focal point of the haunting, which was being caused by the troubled spirit of an old woman. Father Alfred Cole, of St Matthew's, was consulted about exorcism but the proposal was not taken as far as the bishop, whose permission would have been needed.

It appeared that the poltergeist did not find human presence in the building an essential for its performance. The senior Mrs Greenfield told me of a day when, alone in the place, she had gone to do some shopping. When she returned, she found a married daughter and a journalist waiting on the doorstep. They said they had heard loud thumps and sounds of movement from inside the house. When the trio entered, they found heavy furniture had been shifted and a mirror hanging in the hall reversed to face the wall.

The invader also seemed to take periods of rest. There were numerous lulls of varying duration, the longer ones providing the Greenfields with sufficient courage to reoccupy their normal sleeping-quarters. Following one such interval, Cecil telephoned me just after midnight on 12 August and said there had been a renewed outbreak which had just culminated in eight-year-old Gordon being flung down the stairs. Happily, he had escaped injury. Begging me to return to the house at once, Cecil said that household articles were being inexplicably transported upstairs from the kitchen and downstairs from the bedrooms. Dennis had seen a bottle of milk proceeding upstairs of its own volition, one step at a time!

Arriving at the house that evening, I found the ground-floor living-room full of the family and their friends. The Greenfields were preparing for another night of cat naps in their armchairs and on improvised communal beds. In the first-floor front bedroom I was shown a scene of strange disorder. The largest of its three beds, normally occupied by the senior Greenfields, was heaped with books, domestic items and cooking utensils from downstairs. A small table was overturned and the dressing-table was draped with the coverlet from a bed. I was told that the other two beds had been occupied by

Patricia and Cecil, the latter no longer willing to sleep alone in his own room. Downstairs, many things had apparently been disturbed in the kitchen. In the hallway, medicine bottles had been placed in neat rows along the upper ledges of doorframes.

I suggested that the first-floor bedroom be restored to order and put under control. Matters were sorted out and the room was made tidy. I locked the door and pocketed the key at 9.45 p.m. Dennis, his wife, mother-in-law and Gordon went upstairs to their two second-floor rooms. Everyone else returned to the ground-floor living-room.

Patrolling the dark and silent staircase at 10.15, I discovered that the key to the front first-floor room also operated the lock on the door of the back room on that level. I secured both doors and rejoined the family downstairs. Shortly afterwards there were shouts from Dennis that his mother-in-law's bed in the front second-floor room had been disturbed while they were all in the other room. I went up and saw that the bedclothes were slightly disarranged. I straightened them and, finding that the key which locked the two lower bedrooms also fitted that door, secured the unoccupied room. A little later, Dennis called out that the bed on which he had been resting in the top back room had been unaccountably tampered with. This had happened, he said, while he, his wife, his mother-in-law and her boy had all been in the room. They were all white-faced, tense and frightened.

I rechecked each of the locked rooms shortly before leaving the house in the early hours. Everything was normal. Returning the key to the senior Mr Greenfield, I advised everyone to go to their beds, assuring them that I believed that the remainder of the night would pass without trouble. They seemed inclined to accept this advice, which proved correct.

Driving home, I found myself ruminating over my doubts about the statements I had heard from Dennis. He could, I reflected, have several incentives for creating or assisting the disturbances, the departure of his mother-in-law and gaining a larger share of the house being perhaps the most obvious. On the other hand, he was suffering his share of discomfort from the affair, both at home and in respect of the public taunts. And, most significant of all, there had been occasions – particularly during the presence of the police – when he would have needed a Magic Circle degree of skill to have produced the effects by trickery. After a lengthy debate with myself, I decided to catalogue some of his claims as hallucinations arising from the long weeks of strain he and his family had endured. Whether they were deliberate or involuntary, his exaggerations did not, I concluded, destroy the overall validity of the case.

Early in October, Cecil claimed to have been awakened one night to find another spectral figure standing beside his bed. He noticed that it appeared to be offering him some objects which looked like 'pieces of tin'. Terrified, he had dived beneath the bedclothes. When he summoned the courage to peep out again, the figure had vanished. Two days later, the senior Mr Greenfield reported, he had heard a loud noise in the kitchen. There was then no one in that room. When he investigated, he found the heavy kitchen table had been turned round.

I was shown marks that were said to have appeared on the wall of a first-floor bedroom and in the cellar when those places had had no human occupants. I took a tracing of the scratchings in the bedroom. They seemed to read: 'MP S2 [or Z] 38.' No one in the house recognized them as having any meaning. The cellar scratchings were merely a patch of marks at a height where they might have been made by the family's cat or puppy, both of which sometimes visited the place.

The succeeding course of events was typical of the final phase of a poltergeist infestation. The strange noises persisted intermittently for a few more weeks, gradually softening and withdrawing to the point where they had begun – the loft. Then they stopped altogether. The other effects also ceased.

The case possessed what seems to be a common (but by no means essential) ingredient in outbreaks of poltergeist phenomena – the presence of a young person around the age of puberty.

Two years later the Greenfields moved to a new home and were replaced at Langmead Street by young Mr and Mrs E. Hewitt and their four small children. I visited them a year after they moved in. They said they had experienced nothing unusual in the house, which seemed luxurious to them after their previous home in a converted wartime Nissen hut. They knew of the strange events in the building, and their toddlers often called out to 'Horace', as they had named the disturbing entity. But 'Horace' had never given the slightest sign that 'he' had heard their greetings.

Four years after the Langmead Street haunting had made headlines, I visited ex-Inspector Candler – he had then retired after thirty-nine years in the force – at the dockland hostelry where his son-in-law was licensee. He recalled the case with clarity and discussed many of its details with me. He had often thought about it, he said, but his original opinion remained unchanged. 'Nobody could persuade me that adult people would be as terrified as the Greenfields obviously were without having good reason for it. I am satisfied they were not playing tricks. Nobody could go to work all day and then sit up all night playing pranks over a long period like that. What it was I just don't know. It baffled me then and it baffles me still.'

I asked him whether he had ever encountered another case comparable with the Langmead Street poltergeist.

'Never,' he said.

9. Whitechapel Weirdness

The very name of London's Whitechapel, with all its incongruity, calls up visions of wretched warrens, menacing alleyways, spluttering gas-lamps and clip-clopping old horses dragging carts through mean streets. Here were the notorious stews and thieves' kitchens of the Victorian city; here stalwart constables were afraid to patrol alone; here the never-identified 'Jack the Ripper' hacked his woeful victims to death.

Ancient Whitechapel has been swept away. Concrete has replaced crumbling brick; asphalt has succeeded cobblestones; modern lighting has taken over from gas-lamp; the roar of heavy engines has superseded the fall of hoof. Yet still, somewhere in the air, hang the lingering impregnations of yesteryear.

Dress-manufacturer Harry Cox and his wife Brenda moved into 88 Newark Street, Whitechapel, in June 1954. Having served as an infantryman in Palestine, Egypt and Germany from 1943 to 1948, twenty-seven-year-old Cox was eager to prove his entrepreneurial skill in the world of commerce. Sewing machines, cutting tables and clothes-racks were installed in workrooms on the top floor of the four-storey building. Workers were engaged. The Coxes took up residence in a living-room and kitchenette on the first floor and a bedroom on the second. A week later, Doncaster-born Alec Bessell and his shorthand-typist wife Vera moved into the ground-floor flat. Bessell was to be a salesman on the Cox staff. Orders came in, the machines began to hum and the dresses were despatched. Everything seemed set for success.

Then some of his machinists began asking Cox who was playing jokes. He said he did not know what they were talking about. They told him that several times they had heard footsteps mounting the bare wooden stairs towards the door of their room, only to stop just before reaching the final step. Again and again they had run to the stairway hoping to catch the intruder, but they never found anyone there. Cox scoffed. 'You're imagining things,' he told them.

A few days later he began to change his mind. Sitting with his wife in the otherwise deserted house one evening, they both heard distinct footfalls on the stairs outside their room. Thinking that someone had broken in with a view to theft, Cox grabbed a poker and strode out to do battle. The place was empty, the doors were still locked. He and Brenda spent the remainder of the evening trying to explain to themselves how they could have heard footsteps when there was no one on the staircase. But heard them they had – of that they were certain.

A short while after their strange experience the house was left empty one evening when all its residents were out on various errands. But neither of the couples knew that the other was also absent. After returning home at eleven, the Bessells were enjoying a nightcap when they heard some heavy thumps and 'sounds like sweeping noises' from the rooms just above them. Irritated by the thought that it was an inconsiderate hour for housework, they went to bed. They were awakened at 12.30 by the sound of the front door opening and subdued voices in the hallway. Thinking that they were the victims of burglars, Bessell ran to intercept. He found the Coxes newly arrived home. Astonished, he told of the sounds from their rooms. They dashed upstairs. Nothing was displaced.

Worse was to follow. Asleep in their second-floor bedroom at 2.30 one morning in July, Harry and Brenda awoke to feel the clothes being slowly pulled down to the foot of their bed. The room was filled with an icy chill. 'By the time we were fully conscious, the clothes had gone,' Cox told me. 'We put on the light and saw them piled on the floor at the end of our bed. Needless to say, we didn't have any more sleep.' The same thing occurred four times more, always in the dead of night.

Cox tried to continue working normally despite the mounting strain on his nerves. Faced with an inrush of orders, he was pressing dresses in the top floor workroom in the early hours one morning. Brenda and the Bessells were all asleep in their beds. 'Suddenly,' Cox told me, 'I felt myself become transfixed, absolutely rigid with cold, and my hair stood on end. I tried to move but there seemed to be no life in my arms or legs. I have never had such a horrifying experience. After what seemed to be an age I was able to get out of the grip of the thing, whatever it was, and drag myself downstairs.'

There came a period when Bessell's travels in search of sales made it necessary for him to spend nights away from home. To keep Vera company, the Coxes slept in her flat. All three heard heavy crashes from the unoccupied rooms above. After a time they gave up examining the places from which the noises seemed to come – there was never anything unusual to see.

Precisely at midnight on 27 September – the beginning of the Jewish new year of 5715 – the three of them, sitting in the ground-floor flat, heard heavy, measured thumps descend the forty-eight stairs from the top to the bottom of the house. Again, an immediate search produced no explanation. But they decided to remain together through the night. At 12.30 a.m. Cox secured the Yale lock on the only door to the room. No one went near it until 7.30 a.m. – when it was found unfastened. Once, the first-floor living-room door, for which there was then no key, was found locked. Cox had to break in.

On 19 October some friends stayed with the Coxes overnight. Harry slept with twenty-seven-year-old Michael Vinter in the living-room, where a number of dresses and spare coat-hangers were suspended on temporary lines. Next morning Vinter told Cox he had awakened in the night and seen several of the empty hangers spinning round. At the same time he had felt movements on the bed. He had assumed that the effects were caused by Harry moving about. Cox assured me that he had not stirred all night.

Brenda and Vera were greatly frightened by an incident one evening. Sipping tea while talking in Brenda's kitchenette, both saw an artificial flower leap from a vase. It flew towards Vera but stopped before impact, turned diagonally and fell under a table.

Cox told me that the events which alarmed him most were not the bumps in the night but the movements of objects in unoccupied rooms which began soon after the flight of the flower. Having tidied and locked his living-room after working on his books until 2.30 one morning in November, he was the first to enter it later in the day – to find a coloured glass jug and six tumblers from the sideboard laid out on the seats of chairs. In the same room, which was always kept locked when unoccupied, silver cups and medals he and Brenda had won for ballroom dancing were thrown about the floor during the night. On one occasion a vase of water was poured over a pile of income tax forms he had completed before going to bed.

There was a curious happening when a friend called with her dog, which immediately refused to enter the premises. With legs rigid and the hair rising on its back, the animal was pulled into the hallway but would budge no further and bolted back into the street the moment he was released. The only other pet brought into the house was a budgerigar Cox had bought as company for his wife. It showed no signs of discomfort or concern.

Saturday 13 November brought a new turn of events. Harry's parents were visiting. In the afternoon Cox senior was left briefly to himself in the first-floor living-room, listening to the radio. The others were elsewhere in the building. Suddenly Harry's horrified father heard screams – 'like a cat in pain' – burst out in the room. The awesome noises seemed to come from a glass-fronted cabinet at his side. He and Harry searched the room, concentrating on the cabinet. They found nothing to account for the sounds.

I paid frequent calls and spent many hours waiting to catch some hint of the phenomena for myself. I did not succeed. As so often happens, it seemed as though the disturbances were directed by some intelligence that wished to infuriate as well as frighten.

I felt no reason to doubt the accounts I was given by Harry, Brenda, Alec and Vera. As was the case with the Greenfields at Langmead Street, it was apparent that the strange events were causing them considerable psychological stress. Again I considered the element of motivation. There was no question of a desire for improved accommodation being an inspiration for dishonesty. It was also clear that no commercial advantage was to be gained from 'inventing' a poltergeist, there being little inducement for hard-headed wholesalers to purchase clothing made in a 'haunted' factory. In fact, the visitations were obviously doing positive harm. Apart from lack of sleep and wear and tear on nerves, Cox found himself facing a problem that threatened the survival of his new-born business. Frightened by the continuing mystery of the footsteps on the stairs, his machinists began to leave. Like many forms of enterprise, the dressmaking world is something of a village; there was much gossip about the 'haunted workrooms' in Newark Street. Cox found difficulty in replacing the girls who departed.

One of the aspects that I noted was the absence of any young person in the age range that sometimes appears to provide a 'focus' for poltergeist-type outbreaks. Wondering whether there was any 'previous history', I made inquiries. When I contacted the former occupier, Harry Conway, he supplied some interesting information.

Previously unacquainted with the Coxes or the Bessells, Conway told me he and his family had moved out of the house about a year earlier. They had had some horrifying experiences there, he said. Weird events had centred upon and terrified his seven-year-old son, who had occupied a bedroom on the second floor. Night after night the child would scream with terror soon after being put to bed. He always told the same story – that icy fingers had clutched at his face and that the clothes had been slowly drawn off the foot of his bed. Believing the lad to be the victim of childish nightmares, the Conways had done their best to assure him that his fears were just bad dreams. But the troubles had continued, gradually wearing the child down to a nervous wreck. Finally the boy had suffered a total collapse and had to be removed to a mental hospital, where his treatment lasted for several months. It was then that the Conways had decided they must leave the house.

They had, from time to time, heard 'odd noises' about the place, Conway added. For some reason he could not explain, they had not associated the sounds with their son's difficulties. But once an aunt of Conway's had occupied the boy's room and she too had experienced the alarming bedclothes-removing phenomenon. Conway told me he had changed the lock on the boy's room no fewer than seven times during their residence in the house, because the door to that room had constantly been found secured or unfastened without normal cause. Another experience shared by the Coxes.

Introduced by a friend of Harry's, a medium visited the house. I was not present but was told she had 'stumped and staggered' about the rooms and declared that the haunting was caused by the unquiet spirit of a man who had had a wooden leg. At the end of this performance she claimed to have subdued the troublesome spirit and gave an assurance that there would be no more disturbances. This promise proved premature. The noises continued, sporadically, for several weeks more. Then, in typical poltergeist style, they wavered, waned and finally ceased as unaccountably as they had started.

10. Ruby Miller and the Camberwell Palace Ghost

Recollections of London's theatres of variety and music hall now survive mainly in the memories of people above a certain age. By the 1950s most of those moth-eaten palaces of red plush, gilt and greasepaint were dead or dying, swept away by the Luftwaffe, the new brooms of town planners and the cathode ray tube that brought spectacle into the home. During the years of decline the last of the threadbare stages were filled with an incongruous mixture of talents. Female nudity, then considered unpresentable on television, vied with the efforts of old-time performers in the swiftly shrinking world of 'live' show business.

I was fortunate to have the friendship of one of the personalities of the prodigious years of theatre, former 'Gaiety Girl' Ruby Miller. Constantly retelling her tales of flower-filled dressing-rooms and stage-door Johnnies who drank champagne from female performers' slippers, Ruby was always an entertainer.

In 1953 she was appearing at one of London's last-remaining variety halls, the much-battered Camberwell Palace. Her role was as a 'medium' in a play called *Through the Door*, whose plot centred upon a murder mystery that was solved at a seance. The author was ex-actress and former war correspondent Evadne Price, who claimed to have been the first female journalist to enter Belsen concentration camp after its liberation and the first British woman to interview Goering after his capture.

Ruby's experiences in the theatre prompted me to make some inquiries that revealed a background of oddities at the Camberwell Palace. It began, she said, with knocks on her dressing-room door. The play was then in rehearsal. Thinking someone wished to see her, she said 'Come in.' Nothing happened. The knocks came again.

Deciding that her visitor was deaf, she yelled at the top of her voice 'COME IN.' Again nothing. Ruby went to the door, opened it and looked out. There was no one to be seen. She walked down the corridor. There was nobody in any of the adjoining dressing-rooms. 'Everyone else was either on the stage or in the wings,' Ruby explained. 'My first entrance was halfway through the first act. The unaccountable knocks continued, on and off, the entire week. However, the first night passed off without incident.

'The next night I went into the theatre through the front of the house. I paused when I reached the orchestra pit to listen to the pianist, who was playing some music he had written. I complimented him on a charming tango and then walked through the pass-door onto the stage. Before I closed the door I could still hear the pianist, but at the same time I heard an orchestra playing circus music, apparently on the stage.

'Thinking someone was putting records on the panatrope we used in the show, I went across to the panatrope corner. But there was no one about and the panatrope was locked. Yet I could still hear the orchestra playing. And then I detected a faint odour – an animal smell like the sort you get in the lionhouses at the zoo. I was very puzzled. I asked the manager if anyone had a radio backstage or if there was a music store anywhere nearby where one would hear records being played. He said no to both questions. But I went on hearing the circus music and the knockings on my dressing-room door. And with them I got a sense of tragedy and disaster which neither I nor anyone else could explain. As the week progressed, I grew more and more bewildered. I asked the manager to find out whether anyone else had experienced similar things in the building. After questioning many people without result, he came across a man who remembered the Palace from the days when it was a music hall. Asked if he knew any stories connected with it, he said a dreadful tragedy had occurred there in 1902. During a lion-tamer's act, one of the animals mauled the man so severely that he died backstage. Later I found out that he had dressed in the room I was occupying. And the orchestra had always played circus music for his act.'

Ruby attributed the bizarre events to the fact that, every night at the same hour, the play involved her sitting, as the 'medium', in a cabinet on the darkened stage while six other actors sat around a table for the 'seance'. 'It would be little short of miraculous if psychic phenomena did not occur under such conditions,' she said.

Despite our friendship and my personal regard for her, I was sceptical about her story. It is all too easy to lose control of a vivid imagination. It was clearly necessary to visit the Camberwell Palace.

I was received by the manager, a friendly and helpful man named Gilbert Oscroft. The show then being staged was called *Don't Be Shy Girls*. Because of another appointment I was able to spend only an hour looking over the building, but I was introduced to two employees who said they had had strange experiences there. I returned two nights later accompanied by a friend, Derek Shephard, a reporter on a new – and, unhappily, short-lived – daily newspaper called the *Recorder*. After a talk with Oscroft we interviewed the two men who had reported odd encounters.

The first was the theatre's part-time fireman, Alfred Goswell. He assured us that every word of his account was true but asked that his name should not be mentioned in any press report. Rumours about his experience in the theatre had, apparently, reached the ears of fellow-workers at a local factory where he was employed during the day and he had been subjected to some unpleasant ridicule. I promised that there would be no publicity of the sort he feared and he told us his story.

Locking up and extinguishing the lights at 11.15 one night, he said, he was astonished to hear the silence suddenly broken by a single note struck on the grand piano in the orchestra pit. A few seconds later the same note sounded a second time. Thinking that a cat kept at the theatre must have jumped onto the instrument, he went on with his task, working his way downstairs. During his journey the same note was struck four or five times more. Walking through the stalls, he was surprised to see the cat coming into the building through a door opening onto a small backyard. He hastened to the orchestra pit and looked over the rail. The place was deserted. But as he stood there the same note – he was, he told us, no musician so could not say which note it was – had sounded once again. A thorough search of the instrument and its surroundings had revealed no explanation.

His colleague, doorman and night watchman Tom Williams, told us of being alone in the empty theatre one night when, looking down from the circle, he was amazed to see the curtain rising on the stage. He had rushed down to the back-stage area and made a careful check but found no one in the building and nothing to account for the occurrence. All the doors were locked. The curtain was not moved mechanically; it had to be raised and lowered by hand. As I discovered for myself, this involved some physical effort hauling on a rope which moved a heavy, counterweighted pulley arrangement. And to perform the task one had to stand on a platform, reached by a ladder, well up in the flies.

The incident had, it seemed, been literally a curtain-raiser to inexplicable events that night. As Williams stood on the stage, his eye was attracted by a movement in the circle he had left only minutes earlier. While he watched, a pair of glass-panelled doors giving access to the circle bar slowly opened – and gently closed again. 'I could feel myself starting to panic,' Williams told us. 'But I knew that as I was alone in the place nobody would hear me if I screamed or shouted. So I took a grip on myself. I put all the lights on and examined the theatre from top to bottom. I found nothing out of the ordinary, but I telephoned Mr Oscroft and told him what had happened. He didn't believe me at first – told me to take more water with it – but I think he does now.'

Williams spoke of other mystifying experiences, some when the place had been occupied during shows. The most persistent puzzle, he said, arose from the many occasions when, standing taking tickets at the entrance to the gallery, he had heard footsteps approaching along the corridor and then, after preparing to welcome the new arrivals to the audience, found no one there.

Accompanied by Oscroft and Shephard, I made another tour of the building, taking notes and photographs as we went. The old place was typical of the theatrical structures of its day – draughty, rambling and full of the odours of stale beer, old tobacco smoke, disinfectant and dry rot that always seemed to linger in such places. Its declining fortunes were apparent in peeling paintwork, patched seats and worn-out carpets.

Because of my suspicions about reports of ghosts in places of public entertainment – especially those facing hard times – I questioned Oscroft in careful detail. He responded with candour, leaving me with the impression that, having had no personal experience of any oddity, he was not unduly concerned by the reports of those who said they had. He was, however, clearly interested in the possibility of discovering some explanation of the encounters described by Ruby and the two men.

Four months later the theatre was the scene of a near-tragedy. A high-speed roller-skating act called the Jeretz Brothers, performing on a miniature platform ten feet above the stage, had reached the climax of their routine when a serious accident occurred. Spinning in the centre of the tiny rostrum, nineteen-year-old Jack had begun whirling his twenty-five-year-old brother Jimmy at the end of a rope held between his teeth. The swiftly revolving Jimmy had reached Jack's shoulder height when something seemed to affect their sense of balance and both hurtled to the stage below. The curtain rang down and the brothers, both unconscious, were rushed to hospital.

In August 1954 I was contacted by a young journalist named David English, who was then working for the magazine *Weekend Mail*. (He was to become Sir David, the eminently successful editor of the *Daily Mail*.) *Weekend Mail* wanted to publish an article on my activities and were interested in the prospect of an experimental seance at the scene of an alleged haunting. As I was about to arrange something of the sort at the Camberwell Palace, I invited English to attend.

Among the mediums who had participated in my psychical assays was one who showed some particular suitability for 'readings' in cases of haunting and obsession, an Acton housewife named Ena Twigg. Married to a former Navy man, she was a regular worker at the Russell Square headquarters of the Marylebone Spiritualist Association (later the Spiritualist Association of Great Britain). I asked her if she would co-operate in another test, giving her no information as to the case or its location. She agreed.

The experiment was timed for the night of 20 August. We were to arrive just after the final curtain of the evening. I met the *Weekend Mail* photographer, a distinguished cameraman named James Jarche, at his Baker Street flat at nine, and we drove to the Twiggs' semi-detached suburban home in East Acton Lane. Leaving there just after ten, we paused halfway through the journey to blindfold Ena. The remainder of the trip was made in silence and by an indirect route. I kept a close watch on Ena's husband, Harry, to ensure that he relayed no information about our whereabouts to his sightless wife. The car was driven into a yard beside the theatre, and Ena was led through an emergency door into a passageway between stage and dressing-rooms. The blindfold was removed in the wings. The main curtain was down, shutting off any view of the auditorium.

A few scantily clad chorus girls were standing about. *Weekend Mail* wanted some pictures of the showgirls 'welcoming' the medium. Ena's prim facial expression on finding herself surrounded by such pulchritude made a good portrayal of contrasts. In the book on her career – *Ena Twigg, Medium* – by Ruth Hagy Brod, she is recorded as thinking: 'Goodness, what am I doing here in this strange place with these half-naked girls?'

The photographs taken, the stage was cleared except for Oscroft, the Twiggs, English, Jarche and myself. Ena was offered a chair but said she preferred to stand. The experiment began at once. The following is an extract from the notes I made at the time, with subsequent comments on items of the information given.

Twigg: There has been a tragedy or near-tragedy here and the man involved in it either passed through a broken heart or ... help me ... do you know if there used to be a musical director who was here for years and years? I am getting the spirit of a man who was bound up with this theatre. I am going back to days when this used to be a variety theatre. I feel that this theatre has been under a cloud or undergoing a sticky patch. (1) This man is trying to stop some change here. It is either going to be pulled down or something like that. Do you understand?

Oscroft: Yes.

T: I get the name Arthur. You have an office here and lights are being switched on and off. He seems to have lost heart and been thrown on the dump heap. There was some change about 1920. He seems to have ended his time about 1920. There has been an accident here. Somebody has been hurt. (2) Somebody thought it was deliberate. He says to tell you there was something about a hat. There is a smell of fire.

O: The roof was on fire during the war, from incendiary bombs.

T: You have been cutting down something – reducing expenses or something like that.

O: No more than usual.

T: This man says if you will let him help you he will be a good ally. This man needs quite a bit of help because he has not been over very long but he has been tied to the theatre. I am told that we should be able to lay the ghost tonight. He has wanted a mouthpiece and nobody would listen to him. Can you tell me about a piano being played without ... (3) He said 'The Palace.' (4) Do you know about that? There is a narrow passage upstairs; that is where he stays. (5) I am told this place was in existence before the beginning of the century.

O: Correct. (6)

T: There was a lot of drinking about two years ago. There was somebody here who used to drink heavily.

O: Yes, true.

T: They are telling me about somebody falling. There has been an accident. (7)

O: Yes.

T: You have got to do something about this place or it will empty itself. I feel that there was a tragedy here and that he just went to pieces. (8) You have found somebody dead here.

O: Yes. (9)

T: It is two lives mixed up here, a man and a woman. I am being torn to pieces here. (10) He is dead when you get there. (11) You have got two people on your track. (12) It is just as though my throat is on fire. I am going to tell you that you are doing something very wrong. Unwittingly, you are subscribing to some of the phenomena. If you read these notes carefully, you will be able to use them in a way that will help you with the problem. Mr Paul will tell you how that can be done. You have got two shades of red in this theatre. (13)

At Ena's request we moved to the circle. She gave no further information there, beyond saying that she wished to see a spiral staircase somewhere in the building. Oscroft was the only person present who knew of its existence, in a room adjoining his office. I had not seen it. Ena stood at the door, where the test ended.

T: There are swing doors which keep going backwards and forwards. (14) There is something about a curtain being drawn. (15) There is something about a face. He is showing me a bed in your office. You have changed your typewriter.

O: No.

T: But you have changed its position.

O: Yes.

T: You are all right now. For your own mental health and the sake of the people who work in this theatre, just send a little thought out that these people may be released, will you?

Comments

1 There had been a recent local controversy about some of the theatre's advertisements.
2 The Jeretz Brothers?
3 The inexplicable piano-playing heard by Goswell?
4 The theatre opened as the Oriental Palace and was renamed Camberwell Palace in 1899. Ena could not possibly have known the name at the time.
5 The gallery corridor where unaccountable footsteps were heard by Williams?
6 The theatre was built in 1896.
7 Again the Jeretz Brothers? Oscroft's response related to an accident suffered by a former employee.
8 'Translated' reference to injuries suffered by lion-tamer in 1902?
9 An elderly patron died of heart failure in a seat in the circle.

10 The lion-tamer?
11 The old man in the circle was dead when Oscroft was brought to him.
12 Another reference to the lion-tamer and the man who died in the circle?
13 A few seats in the auditorium were new and a brighter shade of red than the old ones. Ena had not seen any of them at the time.
14 The circle bar door movements seen by Williams?
15 The unaccountable curtain rising seen by Williams?

Although the experiment produced nothing which could be said to rule out the possibility that Ena gained information through some form of thought-gathering among those in the test group, she appeared to be right about 'laying the ghost'. There were no more reports of strange happenings in the place.

There was, however, an oddity associated with my preparation of preliminary notes for this chapter. Assembling the facts, I consulted papers I had not touched for more than twenty years. As I had heard nothing of Ruby for a long time and realized that she must be advancing in age, I scribbled a reminder note to check with a mutual friend as to her welfare. The words about her came with unusual difficulty. I felt utterly weary and had to struggle to produce them. Then I switched on the radio for the news – and heard that the 'Gaiety Girl' had gone. She had died at the very time I was finding it so hard to write of her. Just coincidence? Possibly. What author Arthur Koestler called 'synchronicity'? Also possible. But it was one of several 'coincidences' – or 'synchronicities' – that occurred during the writing of this book.

Among my memories of Ruby – she was one of nine children borne by the wife of a Mitcham, Surrey, leather merchant – is her account of a conversation she had with the 'father of wireless', Guglielmo Marconi, aboard his yacht *Elettra* in Cowes harbour.

'He told me,' said Ruby, 'that when he passed on he would try to impress upon the mind of a scientist the way to make an instrument to enable people to communicate with the state beyond death. He said it might take hundreds of years, but he was sure the time would come.'

Having the privilege of friendship with Marconi's widow, the charming Marchesa Maria Christina, and their daughter, the Principessa Elettra, I have enjoyed many conversations about the man whose ingenuity and determination opened the way to the communications marvels of today. There could surely be no one better qualified for the task of bridging the gap between life and death.

Like Ruby, the Camberwell Palace has gone. It was demolished in 1966.

11. Rumpus in Runcorn

As mentioned earlier, there is persuasive evidence that certain poltergeist phenomena, whatever their source, cause or purpose, are sometimes directed by a form of intelligence. The unerring responses to Sir William Barrett's audible signals and unspoken requests at Derrygonnelly (see Chapter 4), with the unfailingly accurate counting of finger movements he concealed inside his pockets, provide a classical example of this freakish acuity.

Other indications of a mischievous nous include elusive conduct when under investigation. And, while the records show many instances of violent destruction of property, sometimes with severe psychological effects on individuals, there is no record of any case in which a poltergeist has inflicted, directly, any serious physical injury on a human being.

An outstanding demonstration of this clear discrimination between property and people occurred in the Merseyside town of Runcorn. It became dramatically apparent when objects hurled at walls dented wood and smashed through plaster, while similar items flung at people caused only minor discomfort. The case was still more remarkable because unaccountable phenomena occurred in four separate homes and represented the only discoverable explanation for the deaths of fifty-three animals.

The outbreak began in a small working-class dwelling – 1 Byron Street. As is often the pattern, it started with gentle, nocturnal knocks in a bedroom. Gradually the sounds grew louder. Soon they became violent thuds. Then furniture was smashed, books were torn up, walls and woodwork pitted and scarred, a ceiling cracked and bedding ripped to pieces. In six weeks the room was a shambles.

The house was the rented home of a sixty-eight-year-old farm worker, Samuel Jones. At the beginning of the disturbances the bedroom was occupied by Jones and his sixteen-year-old grandson John Glynn – whose father had died a few months earlier – sleeping together in a large, iron bedstead, and by Jones' middle-aged sister-in-law Lucy, who slept in a smaller bed with John's eight-year-old sister Eileen. The two other bedrooms were being used by visitors from North Wales and Ellen Whittle, a fifty-nine-year-old spinster lodging at the house. (Miss Whittle died two months later, from injuries sustained in a fall into a disused quarry.)

After two disturbed nights the police were called. They examined the premises, laid traps to catch pranksters, kept several long vigils – and retired defeated.

A dressing-table was the initial focal point. Having provided a sounding-board for intermittent knocks and raps, it next began to rattle its drawers, then to creak and groan and finally to move itself out of position. 'I've lived in this house for thirty-three years and I've had the dressing-table for forty-two years,' Jones told a local journalist. 'It never did anything crazy like this before.' He invited the newspaperman to inspect and try to move it. 'It was a good, old-fashioned, hefty piece of workmanship,' the reporter wrote. 'It was heavy.'

After the departure of the perplexed police, Philip France, a Spiritualist medium living in Runcorn, was called to the house. He arranged a three-hour-long seance which was attended by Glynn and his grandfather. Two Bibles, a picture book, a tin of ointment and the table cover were thrown violently, at the same instant, to different parts of the room. France told the awed sitters that the commotion was being caused by the earthbound spirit of John's father, who had 'inadvertently picked up an evil poltergeist connection'. Having relayed a message for the widow, he said that the troubled spirit had been 'released'; further manifestations were unlikely. How wrong he was!

There was, however, a ten-day pause. Then the pixilated dressing-table resumed its antics. Wrote a *Runcorn Guardian* reporter: 'In the small hours, the "ghost" – or whatever it was – threw a clock, with several small articles, five feet across the bedroom in my presence.'

At the request of the residents, he had agreed to spend the night on the living-room sofa. Ten minutes after the household had settled down to sleep, he was called to the 'haunted' bedroom by the urgent voices of Glynn and Lucy Jones. He saw that the dressing-table was moved out from the wall. Mrs Jones refused to remain in the room, so he stretched out on the small bed, his head about two feet from the dressing-table. Samuel Jones and Glynn were in the large bed.

> A few minutes after the lights went out I heard the dressing-table being dragged across the floor [he reported]. When I shone my torch on it, it had not moved. The lights were again extinguished and at about one a.m., with a sudden noise, the clock, a handkerchief, one of two sleeve bands and one of two runners on the table were hurled to the floor. The clock was found on its face beneath one of the beds five feet away, the glass unbroken. A picture book and two bibles on the dressing-table had also been moved a considerable distance, the book remaining balanced on the edge. The sound of the falling clock resembled not so much a throw as an incredibly swift movement lifting it from the dressing-table and placing it on the floor. Whatever it was that moved those things was no living person that I could discover, and I was very close at the time.

The *Runcorn Guardian* did a professional job on the story, publishing a lengthy article reviewing some historical poltergeist infestations. It also gathered some local opinions, ranging from 'Rubbish!' exclaimed by an eighty-two-year-old lady to 'Definitely something supernormal about it' from a younger female. Activities at the local Spiritualist church were described, with details of larger organizations in the field and explanations of some Spiritualist terminology. Runcorn ministers of orthodox faiths were said to be 'almost unanimous in their comments on ghosts and spirits insofar as the possibility of their existence is concerned'.

After another respite lasting just over two weeks, there was a sudden, forceful flare-up. Quickly on the scene, two *Runcorn Guardian* reporters recorded the facts under headlines reading ' "Ghost" Gives Vent to Violent Temper: Furniture Smashed in Six-Hour Battle':

> Members of the Jones and Glynn families again had their peace shattered on Saturday night, when the 'ghost' returned with redoubled violence. On Sunday, in the presence of seven neutral observers, it smashed furniture and subjected the watchers to a steady bombardment of books, drawers and small articles for six hours. Earlier the same night, 'it' had followed the youth, John Glynn, to his mother's home at 116 Stenhills Crescent, Runcorn, where it manifested itself through minor phenomena in the form of raps on doors and windows. At Byron Street, furniture in the middle bedroom had been moved around in the hope of keeping the then-quiet poltergeist in a permanent state of inactivity, but to no avail. Saturday night saw a start with the gentle turning over of a book on the dressing-table, which now stood by the window, but the

manifestations rapidly became more violent; the dresser was heavily thrown about; a chair was thrown with tremendous force against a wall; a heavy blanket chest at the head of the smaller bed in the position originally occupied by the dressing-table began to 'dance'; the clock on the dressing-table was hurled to the floor, this time breaking the glass, and a carpet was thrown from one side to the other.

On Sunday two *Guardian* representatives with Mr R W Brown (a member of the Chester Society for Psychical Research and an employee at Castner-Kellner Works), Mr Frank Watson, 6 Byron Street, Runcorn, and Mr Johnny Bury, 4 Picow Street, Runcorn, kept watch for six hours; they were joined at irregular intervals by Mrs E Dowd, 26 Granville Street, Runcorn, and by a Mrs Lilian Bailey of Cadishead. Throughout the night they were subjected to a constant, violent and at times dangerous bombardment, with an assortment of hard objects, while John Glynn and Johnny Bury were both, themselves, thrown about the room.

First indication of 'the presence' was the lifting and dropping of the blanket chest – weighing well over half a hundredweight – with a resounding bang. Then books, a torch, a jar of ointment, a cigarette case and other similar objects from both chest and dressing table followed each other in a mad career about the room at incredible speed. Chunks of plaster were dislodged from the walls and a water jug and basin were smashed. The long-suffering clock on the dressing table had its glass and front removed and placed on the table top while the clock itself was thrown to the floor. Everything movable was hurled from the top of the dresser and the chest. Then things really began to move. First the dressing table then the blanket chest were rattled, banged, rocked and lifted from the floor. When lifted they were not merely dropped again but thrust down with great force, causing plaster to fall from the ceiling of the room below and resulting in a wide crack across one corner. The noise was deafening. The chest was banged repeatedly against the end of the bed on which the four male watchers were seated, with sufficient force to move it, and invisible hands grasping Johnny Bury (who shared the double bed with John Glynn) by the pyjamas, pulled him forcibly to the floor.

After this a *Guardian* reporter sat on the blanket chest. There was some activity from the dresser on the far side of the double bed but none from the chest, whereupon he remarked 'I've foxed it this time. It can't move the chest with me on it!' He was immediately struck violently about the head and shoulders with four books in quick succession, hurled from the dressing table, but retained his position with the comment that the chest was still immobile. Two small drawers then whistled past his head and smashed to pieces on the wall behind him, scattering the contents over the remaining three men on the small bed. Mrs Dowd then joined the watchers with the innocent remark 'I don't think it will throw anything at me.' Within seconds she received a heavy volume of

Shakespeare's works full in the face for an answer. Soon afterwards she left the room, but returned at irregular intervals and on every occasion something was thrown at her. Meanwhile, each time books and articles were replaced on dresser or chest they were as quickly hurled off again and heavy movements of the furniture would begin.

The bed, with the three men sitting on it, was suddenly pulled from the wall. The chest continued 'dancing' vigorously in one corner and the dressing table continued to rock, often at the same time as the chest now, in a crescendo of sound that made speech impossible. Once only the movement of the dressing table was caught in the beam of a torch. It was rocking perilously back and to and continued thus three times before it stopped – quite suddenly – in a fraction of a second as though suddenly realising the light was shining upon it.

John Glynn, now growing used to the phenomena apparently manifesting through him, courageously took a turn on the girating [sic] blanket chest. A startled 'Ooooo-oh! What in the world's happening?' brought several torches to life, to reveal John removed bodily from the chest and deposited across the knees of his grandfather, Sam Jones, who had stationed himself at the foot of the double bed.

Thereafter, all 'ammunition' was removed from both dressing table and chest so the thing, concentrating its venom on the dressing table, promptly proceeded to smash it piece by piece. It started by removing one wing and the mirror with a resounding crash. Next, the two large single drawers were removed and thrown across the room, just missing the heads of John Glynn and John Bury. The remaining wing crashed to the floor, the fronts of the two double drawers, too tightly jammed in to be pulled out, were bashed inwards. The joints in the woodwork began to give way and panels from the back were ripped off, all to the accompaniment of furious and rapid banging of the blanket chest against the end of the smaller bed.

During the last hour, to add to the torment, the occupants of the double bed repeatedly had their pillows snatched from beneath their heads and, if they held on, they were themselves dragged across the bed. The bedclothes were time and again whisked off their bodies and deposited elsewhere, usually round some watcher's head. Almost exactly at six am the phenomena ceased abruptly. No-one had slept – but seven respectable, independent witnesses had endured unforgettable experiences.

The Reverend W.H. Stevens, of Wesley Church, Widnes, a member of the Society for Psychical Research, visited the house with the Reverend Kinsey Lester of Hartland Methodist Church, Widnes. The *Runcorn Guardian* reported Stevens as saying: 'I don't think there is any evidence that it is a Spiritistic or other-worldly influence.

It centres round a boy of 17 and is caused, I believe, by an excessive vitality in young people which is released through a strata [sic] of the unconscious mind.' Stevens' opinion of John Glynn was: 'A likeable young fellow, not a shifty type who might arouse suspicion, but a frank, open young man with a straightforward manner, to whom I took immediate liking.'

'Mr Stevens believes the key to the whole matter is an understanding of the human personality,' the paper declared. ' "If we really understood our faculties, a great many things would be cleared up," he affirmed. He pointed out that, while we have normal faculties, we also possess supernormal faculties that are inexplicable to the human mind with present limited knowledge. As an example, Mr Stevens quoted the link between mind and matter. "That is a mystery we still cannot explain," he said, "although we accept it as a quite normal faculty. In this case," he suggested, "we are dealing with supernormal faculties, which are an even greater mystery, in which a personal force without any physical contact raises material objects." '

The report continued with an account of the minister's experience in the restless bedroom:

> Equipped with a torch, Mr Stevens stayed in the darkened room, the boy lying on the bed. With him was Mr Lester and another investigator in no way connected with the family, who sat on the edge of the bed between the boy and a large, heavy box which could be lifted but which would be difficult to carry.
>
> The noises began. A dictionary flew across the room and hit Mr Stevens on the head. Soon, vibrations rocked the dressing table. Mr Stevens switched on his torch and in its light the furniture was still vibrating violently. Later the heavy box moved and then turned over. The man on the bed sat on it, but it continued vibrating and lifted him slightly off the floor. Books were hurled about and a clock was thrown against the wall and shattered.
>
> 'While the dressing table was moving,' said Mr Stevens, 'I asked this force, whatever it is, 'If you can hear me, knock three times.' There was an immediate response, the dressing table shaking violently three times. 'I shone my torch and still it rocked,' he added. He said no-one touched it and only some supernormal, yet not supernatural, force could be responsible. He intends to apply further tests, but believes that as in other similar cases, it may go on for some time then gradually peter out, never to return.
>
> Mr Lester said 'I must confess I went as a sceptic, but at the time I had no open mind. Strange things did happen, but I do not feel inclined to

make any definite statement until I have weighed the matter up.' Mr Lester said that he had a torch and also had his hand on the light switch. When he switched on after the noises started the dressing table was going full tilt, and all present saw it moving.

The *Runcorn Guardian* editorial opinion, published in the same issue, was unequivocal:

> The manifestations at Byron Street this week have reached proportions that settle any dispute as to their reality. Too many independent witnesses have been present, on too many occasions – apart from our own representatives. Two psychic researchers (a body of investigators well known for their logical, not to say sceptical, approach), three Methodist ministers and at least two police officers are among these witnesses. Phenomena has [sic] occurred in the presence of all these witnesses under conditions precluding the possibility of fraud without their connivance. On Monday night, for instance, our own experience tells of movement in the light of a torch. This was repeated on Tuesday in the presence of three ministers of religion and a psychic researcher.
>
> Lights were flashing on and off at any time and in any direction; anyone fraudulently producing phenomena would almost certainly have been discovered and movements sometimes occurred which simply could not have been produced by normal means without the connivance of the watchers – usually a different group each night. The evidence seems overwhelming and though to speculate on the cause is natural, to deny the reality of the occurrences is merely to brand intelligent men and women as either liars or fools.

The following week the paper reported that the strange happenings at Byron Street had been seen by some sixty people. The opinion of representatives of the Methodist, Church of England, Presbyterian and Catholic faiths was said to be that:

> Almost to a man, each agreed to the possibility (in some cases the probability) of such phenomena resulting from the activity of evil spirits. These opinions cannot be discounted.
>
> Two alternatives remain – the Spiritualist explanation of a discarnate personality (not necessarily evil) seeking communication for some definite purpose, and that which has so far gained widest credence, the existence of an unknown force, possibly of subconscious origin, emanating from the human personality of, in this case, John Glynn.

After presenting some mediumistic theories, the writer added:

> On one occasion this week, heavy furniture was moved in all four corners of the room at the same time and activity was seen in torchlight, and

> books and small articles were thrown while the electric light was burning. Local Spiritualists tried to contact the cause of the incidents on two nights last week by holding seances at Byron Street. At the first, when seven 'sitters' and two independent watchers were present, there were no supernormal activities but two male mediums are reported to have gone into trances during which they spoke in a language unintelligible to the others present, but believed to be similar to that of some African tribes. A code of raps was used at the second seance and the medium, it is stated, made contact with the spirit of an African native who said he, his wife and six children had been murdered by members of his own tribe. The spirit gave the name 'Jooker' and said his tribe was the Impis. He wanted no help from anyone present; he was a worshipper of the devil, hated the Bible. He declared he intended to persist in the production of destructive phenomena for a long time.

Assisted by the Reverend J.L. Stafford, the Reverend Stevens attempted some tests aimed at eliminating fraudulence. The *Runcorn Guardian* described the results:

> John Glynn was seated on a chair in the centre of the floor right away from the dressing table while Mr Stafford held his left shoulder, leaving the arm free for protection of his face against flying objects, and a Mr Thompson of Picow Street, Runcorn, held his right arm and hand in a firm grip; Johnny Bury was lying on the centre of the large double bed – out of reach of the furniture on either side of him; other witnesses stood on the far side of John Glynn and no person, with the exception of Johnny Bury, were [sic] between him and the dressing table. Under these circumstances, movements of the dresser on one side of the bed and of the chest on the other, followed each other repeatedly with such rapidity as to be almost simultaneous; it is unlikely Johnny Bury, on the bed, could have turned from side to side at sufficient speed to produce this effect or alternatively, were this possible, his movements must have been so violent as to attract attention. On another occasion phenomena occurred with John Glynn seated on the single bed, with four solid independent witnesses in front of him.
>
> On Friday night Mr Stevens imposed test condition unknown to the rest of the watchers. A number of small articles, among them a jig-saw puzzle, were placed on the dressing table for 'ammunition' and after this was done, when no-one was looking, Mr Stevens changed the position of the jig-saw. As the lights were extinguished, the only person within reach of the dresser was John Glynn, who was well tucked-up in bed with his hands under the covers. He [Stevens] had noticed much of the throwing phenomena to be preceded by a slight clicking sound so, torch at the ready, as soon as he heard this sound he switched on. The beam of his torch caught the jig-saw puzzle just commencing its flight but, most

important of all, it also caught John Glynn, the only person who could possibly have been responsible, still lying swathed in bedclothes with his arms beneath him.

As was the case with the poltergeist outbreak at West Norwood, the events at Byron Street attracted human attentions that were as unwelcome as the inexplicable turmoil. The *Runcorn Guardian* mentioned the problem in an editorial headed 'Unseemly':

> Disturbances in Byron Street, so much in prominence these recent weeks, have not been confined entirely to those of a supernormal order. On Thursday last week an attempt was made to alleviate the conditions there by a Spiritualist seance, which proved exceedingly difficult because of the behaviour of a large number of people outside the house, banging and shouting for entry. Regardless of one's views on the value of such seances, behaviour of this sort cannot be countenanced. Some of the strangers were so overbearing in their demands for admission, it was fortunate police officers were in the house. This deliberate intrusion into the privacy of a family already sufficiently distressed has been repeated. Prompted by little more than idle curiosity and little or no desire to help, such behaviour is quite unwarrantable.

With the primary effects concentrated at Byron Street and following the minor mysteries that had pursued Glynn to his parental home, there was next an extraordinary occurrence when John and his strongly built nineteen-year-old friend John Bury were lunching at the Kingsley, Cheshire, residence of a Widnes businessman – the third house to become involved in the sequence of oddities.

The businessman, Clifford Davies, owner of a vehicle tyre concern with depots in Widnes and Northwich, was also a member of the Society for Psychical Research. He had followed events at Byron Street with interest, visiting the house on a number of occasions. Eager to observe Glynn away from his disrupted environment, he invited him to lunch at his home. John accepted, with the condition that Bury should accompany him.

The youths were collected by car and driven to Davies' home, a converted farmhouse some eight miles from Runcorn. Six people were present for lunch, which was taken in the large kitchen – Davies, his wife Joan, his elderly mother, the Davieses' five-year-old daughter Margaret and the two Johns. The host sat at the head of the table, with his daughter facing him at the foot. Bury sat next to Davies, on his left, Glynn sat next to the little girl, on Davies' right. The chair between Bury and the child was to be occupied by Joan

Davies, and that between Davies and Glynn by the host's mother who, at the time of the incident, was seated a little behind and to the right of her son, by a window.

Serving the meal, Joan went to a cupboard on her husband's left and, from a new, pint bottle, poured a glass of lemonade for Bury, which she handed to him at the table. She was pouring a second glass, for Glynn, when there was a sound like a small explosion and the glass burst in her hand, inflicting slight cuts to her index finger and thumb. The written report Davies later supplied to me reads:

> She was facing at about right angles to John Glynn so that she was, in effect, pouring out the liquid in the opposite direction to him. Looking down, I saw that the glass she had held was shattered and the lemonade bottle empty. The glass was a very thick one and of poor quality.
>
> On looking up I saw John Glynn standing up and he was dripping wet, his hair down over his face and his shirt and coat wet also. In addition, the chair on which he had been sitting had distinct pools of liquid on it. There was no trace of moisture on the table cloth, none on any other person or, as far as I could see, the floor covering of coconut matting except for one small patch on the arm of my jacket.
>
> Being very puzzled as to the cause of this, I took out a single glass from the cupboard and dropped this from various heights into the floor – coconut matting over asphalt. The glass did not break but merely bounced and I could not break it even dropping it from about 8′ 6″.
>
> This occurrence was witnessed by myself, my wife, John Bury, my five-year-old daughter. My mother who was also in the room was sitting in the window knitting – she did not hear the glass 'explode' because, presumably, of indifferent hearing, but she could bear witness to the results.

Joan Davies also supplied me with a signed testimony, reading: 'I declare that the statement recently made by my husband concerning the occurrences when John Glynn of Runcorn visited this house is entirely true and correct. The only feeling I had was one of surprise and astonishment.'

A diagram accompanying Davies' report indicated that, at the time of the mysterious 'explosion', his wife was some six or seven feet away from Glynn, with the table between them. It would have been impossible for her to have thrown the entire contents of glass and bottle simultaneously over her young guest with such accuracy, at the same time ensuring that none of the lemonade fell on the intervening table or floor.

Two nights later, a Sunday, the two Johns suffered another onslaught in the much-plagued bedroom. They occupied the large bed while another friend of Glynn's, Dennis Fallon, of Norleane Crescent, Runcorn, took the small one. Reported the vigilant *Runcorn Guardian*:

> Parts of the broken dressing table were used to belabour the three lads in turn; John Glynn has two large bumps on his head as evidence. 'It' transferred its attention to Dennis Fallon. He was beaten about the arms, raised to protect his head. The piece of wood with which he was being struck continued, apparently suspended in mid-air, to rain blows upon him in the light of an electric torch. The pillow which he interposed was snatched from his hands and ripped. Feathers scattered about the room. Later the same night, with only three boys in the room, furniture moved in all four corners practically simultaneously. The ill-fated dressing table, which had been placed upside down for safety, was lifted from the floor and dropped on to John Glynn and Johnny Bury in the double bed; in a third corner a marble-topped wash stand was moved nearly three feet out from the wall; in the fourth corner the single bed, with Dennis still lying on it, was overturned, burying him under a mountain of mattress and feathers from which he crawled only with the greatest difficulty. All these things happened within seconds of each other.
>
> Downstairs, meanwhile, half-deafened by the noise, were Mr and Mrs Ned Jones, 7 Weir Street, Lower Walton, Warrington, relations of the family; Sam Jones who by this time had had enough of it upstairs; Mrs Lucy Jones; Mrs Elizabeth Jones (another relation) of Ivy Street, Runcorn; and John's mother Mrs Glynn with her daughter Winnie.
>
> Earlier, the entity performed in the presence of three young police officers. They were provided with a display involving movement of furniture and the hurling of books and other articles about the room. By means of knocks indicating the letter of the alphabet 'it' required, these officers were each correctly told their initials, though these had not been divulged. Twice the 'thing' got them right at the first attempt. With the third man it was successful at the fourth attempt. The officers left the house sorely puzzled.
>
> Immediately the light was again extinguished, the phenomena redoubled in violence. Drawers from the dresser hit John on the head, were broken by the impact. Johnny Bury was lifted from bed and dumped behind the dresser; later John Glynn was lifted and deposited in the upturned dresser and seconds later Johnny Bury was dropped behind him, the two being crammed in back to back! Johnny Bury, sitting hunched up on the bed, had a large single drawer smashed over his

knees. A piece of the drawer, 18 inches long, six inches wide, an inch thick, was later used to belabour Dennis Fallon.

In its issue for the following week the paper published an article headed 'John Glynn Tells What It's Like To Live With a Ghost.' What, it queried, were the feelings of a youth who, for two months, had been in touch with things he didn't understand? A reporter said to have had no previous contact with John or Byron Street contributed a pen-picture:

> They say you can get used to anything. John has grown accustomed to the strange activity which seems to surround him. When the violence and noises began, he was terrified. His heart thumped against his ribs, he felt cold, bed-time became a thing to be dreaded. But, gradually, he has adopted the most sensible attitude of all. He does not know what this force is but does not take it too seriously. He laughs about it, calls it 'Jooker,' 'Brutus' and 'It.' He has got used to being pointed out as the 'ghost boy,' to receiving anonymous letters with offers of help, to being stopped in the street to discuss 'Jooker' with strangers. He confesses to a 'funny feeling' somewhere in his tummy when he goes to bed wondering whether there is going to be any rest for him that night. John was christened in the Roman Catholic Church but was brought up by his grandfather as a Protestant. John's father wasn't too keen about that. When the Roman Catholic priest visited Byron Street, his friendliness left John greatly comforted and more able to bear the strange violence. At the moment he is off work so that he can catch up on those sleepless nights when 'It' gave no peace to him or anyone else in the room. John doesn't like having time off. He likes his job – a clerical one – and wants to get back.
>
> John's friends scoffed when the experiences began. Dour Johnny Bury volunteered to share John's bed. The violence began and as the lads huddled under the bedclothes, subjected to a rain of blows, John asked 'Do you believe me now, Johnny?' 'I don't know what to think,' said the muffled voice beside him.
>
> John's life has followed the pattern of hundreds of boys of his age. I think his intelligence is above average. He told me he was good at mathematics and English during his school days. The combination is unusual. I found him sincere, bright, easy to get on with, a comfortable sort of bloke to talk to. There were no awkward pauses in our conversation, whether it was about 'Jooker' or the latest films. In short, John is a lad with strong, likeable personality. I took to him, as the saying goes, right from the start. He has a girl friend, is fond of dancing, likes a game of snooker or billiards, plays a mouth organ and reads Western novels. I should think he has lots of friends. He is that kind of boy, a boy not given to moods and introspection. I'm fond of snooker too. I took John for a game, but neither of us played very well. 'What a pity

old Jooker can't play for me,' John commented laughingly. And that, I thought, summed up his attitude pretty well. John doesn't intend to let 'It' get him down.

The feature was accompanied by an account of the previous week's events:

> Runcorn's 'ghost' is still active at 1 Byron Street and has evidently now become at least partially independent of John Glynn, on whom the phenomena has [sic] so far centred almost entirely. A book has been thrown from the unoccupied middle bedroom in the house. Other phenomena occurred when John Glynn was not in the house. When a camera was introduced into the room the phenomena ceased. Phenomena continued after John Glynn returned to bed, but at infrequent intervals. All attempts to obtain a photograph failed. Pieces of the dresser, now almost wrecked, were thrown about so violently that paint on the door connecting the middle bedroom with one at the back was marked, and in one place the wood bears an indentation nearly a quarter of an inch deep. A book hit John Glynn in the corner of his left eye and bruised the skin; his eye was still discoloured more than 24 hours later. In answer to a cry for help from the two boys, left alone, Sam Jones went up to investigate. The clothes and mattress from the single bed had been thrown over them. On these the top of the broken dresser had been dropped. Finally, a broken leg from the dressing table was clubbing the table top.

There were some amusing side-effects from the disturbances. The congregations at local churches increased, in one establishment reaching the largest numbers seen since the long-serving vicar had taken up the incumbency. Attendances at nearby Spiritualist meetings were also boosted, as was interest in a series of Christadelphian lectures.

The readers' letters columns of the neighbourhood Press were filled with debates about the weird invader. A Bible student declared that a demon was at work, adding that theories about unknown forces were 'a useful refuge for the atheistically-minded' and, oddly, affirming that the hypothesis of a discarnate personality was 'based on the fallacy that man has an immortal soul'. The letter warned: 'Demonism thrives on darkness. That is probably why the spirits of your accounts take such a violent dislike to the Bible. The most fraudulent of these "lying wonders" is the imitation of certain characteristics of persons who have died, thereby deceiving many people into thinking they have been communicating with their loved ones "on the other side". This is why the Bible strongly condemns

Spiritism (Leviticus 19:31; Deuteronomy 18: 10-12; 1 Chronicles 10:13; Isaiah 8:19-20; Revelation 22:15 &c).'

These views were quickly challenged. A writer describing himself as 'a member of the Christadelphian Auxiliary Lecturing Society' expressed concern that the happenings were being explained as the work of evil spirits – 'deceiving your readers by mis-quoting from the Bible. The Bible knows nothing of a supernatural Devil, nor of any once-perfect, but rebel, spirits.' He ended with an appeal: 'Let us allow the Bible to "make us wise unto Salvation" and not misuse it to bolster up the theories of pagan philosophers as so many, including your letterwriter, do.'

Another correspondent likened the scriptures to a weapon: 'The Bible at 1 Byron Street, which seems to have suffered so much abuse, is like unto a shining sword which has been left behind by a retreating warrior and is now being trampled down by an advancing foe. To those who wish an interpretation of this I would say: Pick up this sword; use it *rightly* and the DEMON will dispersed' [sic].

Someone else had evidently suffered personal approaches in consequence of stating his views. Quoting from the First Epistle of St Paul to the Corinthians: ' … the manifestation of the Spirit is given to every man to profit withal. For to one is given … the word of wisdom … to another the word of knowledge … to another … faith … to another the gifts of healing … to another the working of miracles … *to another discerning of spirits*,' he ended: 'May I ask that no more come knocking at my door to take up this argument; *my* time is taken up by trying to live out the teaching of the Bible, not by arguing about it.'

Disgruntlement even broke out among the Press. The *Runcorn Weekly News*, rival of the *Runcorn Guardian*, was upset when, for some reason, Samuel Jones ordered its representatives out of the house. 'What is the secret of No 1 Byron Street, Runcorn? What is the tenant, Mr Sam Jones, hiding?' it asked in a front page article. Explaining the questions, the item went on:

> With the object of helping the Jones family and of giving the public a sober account of the mysterious happenings at Byron Street, the *Weekly News* has endeavoured to carry out investigations into the reported manifestations of ghostly activity at the house but has been unable to carry out the most important test of all because Mr Jones would not permit representatives of the paper to stay in the house.
>
> On Wednesday night two *Weekly News* representatives were admitted to the house, together with a party of Runcorn Spiritualists who were

permitted to conduct a seance in the room which is alleged to be the centre of the strange activity. Afterwards the two newspapermen were discussing the happenings at the house with a Widnes businessman and the Rev J L Stafford when Mr Jones came through from another room and ordered the journalists out. This followed an occasion earlier in the week when two reporters were turned away from the house after Mr Jones had told them he could not promise they would be admitted then or at any other time. In spite of his cavalier dismissal of the press on Wednesday night, Mr Jones had no hesitation in admitting several people who were obviously complete strangers to him. One inquisitive visitor who is understood to have been connected with Spiritualist publications, and who admitted he is a believer in psychic phenomena, was allowed to stay in the house when others who had no connection with Spiritualism were turned away. The treatment meted out to *Weekly News* representatives at Byron Street was in direct contrast to the reception given them by Runcorn Spiritualists earlier in the evening.

The nightly human commotion continued outside the house. The *Runcorn Weekly News* report added:

It is understood that some of the neighbours are to prepare a petition asking that the police should disperse the crowd of 'sightseers' who have been congregating in the locality. They are doing this on the grounds that the noise created in the street is preventing them from going to sleep. Letters on this theme have been received by the *Weekly News* this week. One suggests that all the lights should be left burning in the house all night. 'To pay for it,' writes one reader, 'a collection could be made from the large, noisy crowd who swarm round the place every night.'

An octogenarian correspondent has sent a novel letter – completely in shorthand. He writes: 'If they would keep a small lamp burning in the bedroom the ghost would be afraid to come in the night. But would it not deprive you of "copy"?'

The *Weekly News* was not totally disadvantaged in the matter of the strange manifestations. Its income was supplemented by a large advertisement showing two wide-eyed 'phantoms' under a 'Byron Street' road sign, the whiter of the two forms remarking to its greyish companion: 'I use the new launderette in Church Street.'

But the paper was admonished in a *Runcorn Guardian* editorial:

Last week the *Weekly News* attacked Mr Sam Jones, the occupier of No 1 Byron Street, Runcorn, scene of the recent poltergeist manifestations, alleging he had something to hide and had ordered newspapermen off the premises on two separate occasions. In a churlish and ill-tempered article, our contemporary has perpetrated that greatest of all untruths –

> namely, a half-truth – because the only newspapermen ordered off the premises have been members of the *Weekly News* staff. ... The full facts have been available to the public through our newspaper. ... The *Weekly News* comments, written it seems with the juice of sour grapes, fall below professional standards of accuracy and decency. ...

No doubt wishing to preserve as much peace as possible, Jones readmitted the *Weekly News* to his home. The paper recorded that its man had been treated with 'every courtesy'. Jones' decision would, it said, be 'generally welcomed and will allay those suspicions, widely aroused, that unbiassed, factual and objective reporting was not welcome at Byron Street'. The reporter added that, during his visit, he had not witnessed 'a single instance of the type of manifestation which it is said has succeeded in wrecking furniture and damaging the room'. However, 'the lack of activity did not suggest that previous happenings in the bedroom were not as described by reliable witnesses. Instead, the fact that nothing happened strengthened reliability of this evidence, for had there been any trickery the perpetrator of the tricks would almost certainly have arranged a performance for the benefit of the press.'

Despite the non-performance of the poltergeist, the report had other value. It quoted Jones as saying that, unless events made it impossible, he was determined to continue living in the house, which had been his home for nearly forty years. There was, it appeared, no question of 'phenomena' being imagined or created with the aim of securing better housing. 'Repairs to the damage caused as a result of the manifestations will involve Mr Jones in considerable cost,' the *Weekly News* commented, 'but he says it is no good starting repairs before he is assured the work will not be undone.'

All was not quite over. Spending a night in the single bed and accompanied in the room by Glynn and the Reverend Stafford, the chairman of Nantwich Urban Council, H.W. Jones, reported pressure on the blanket covering his legs 'as though the five fingers of a partly-closed hand were pushing. I had the light switched on and asked another person in the room to move further away from the bed. The light was again switched off and three times more I felt the movement of a hand against the blanket, but no-one in the room could have touched it. However, whatever it was, it was very weak.'

Asked for his opinion of the cause of the troubles, Councillor Jones said:

> In my view it is an evil form and those of us who are Christians know

> that if there is a God then there must equally be a devil. We believe God can manifest Himself in a quiet way but the devil must adopt showmanship. This is showmanship. It would appear that the presence of a member of Holy Orders in the bedroom is bringing comfort to John and the manifestations are not now so great. It is the force of God conquering that of evil. My theory is that the weakening of the manifestations is because of the power of good. If a fuller belief in God is acquired, then I am convinced this evil spirit will be defeated and peace will once again reign supreme.

A Manchester-based BBC features producer, Denis Mitchell, compiled a programme of interviews with the residents and other witnesses of the strange effects. A brief attempt to record the sounds of disturbance failed, as had efforts to photograph the poltergeist at work. The broadcast ended with Mitchell's conclusion: 'It is certainly a very odd business.'

Three months after the outbreak began, the disrupting energies were spent. The effects slowly petered out, a tremulous silence returned to the battered house, the nightly crowds ceased to assemble and the newspaper stories began to be forgotten in the hurly-burly of living. Only the residents in the afflicted home, and those who had spent restless hours observing 'impossible' occurrences, retained memories bulging with unanswered questions.

Occupied in London and elsewhere, I was unable to visit Runcorn during the run of the phenomena. I was, however, kept informed of day-to-day events by a journalist colleague, Alan Walker, who was working in Manchester.

Shortly after I had discussed the subject of ghosts on a BBC television programme, I received, via a Sunday newspaper which had commented on the item, a letter from Clifford Davies, the Widnes businessman whose home had been the scene of the 'lemonade incident'. He wrote of his ability to confirm, as an eye-witness, many of the Byron Street oddities. His letter added: 'It is just possible that you may be acquainted with, although I do not think it likely, a further even more extraordinary story concerning a prominent and respected Runcorn farmer who had been associated with the Jones family at 1 Byron Street for many years. If his story is to be believed, and I do believe it, his experiences make the happenings at 1 Byron Street look a little pale by comparison.'

Tantalizingly, the letter added:

> I am not at liberty to say anything about it because the farmer's wife has

a horror of publicity of any sort and the story is so fantastic that I can well understand extreme reticence in even discussing it. If it is true, and apart from knowing the people well the story that they tell is just too fantastic to be invented, then almost certainly it would give a cause and reason and pattern to everything that happened from the beginning of autumn to, I think, the night of 7 December last when the entity very appropriately rolled up the carpet.

I believe it is so big as to make history in the subject and if you are sufficiently interested to come north I think I could arrange for you to meet most of the people concerned, including the farmer and his wife, providing you would undertake not to publicize anything without their consent.

I travelled north at the first opportunity, enjoyed warm hospitality at Clifford and Joan Davies' comfortable home and was given details of astonishing events that had preceded and coincided with the Byron Street outbreak but no word of which, for reasons that will be explained, had reached the Press or public ear.

A well-built, bluff and hearty extrovert Lancastrian in his forties, Davies talked enthusiastically about the strange scenes he had witnessed, accompanying his tale with some alarming both-hand gestures, as he drove us into Runcorn. We spent an hour in the 'focal point' middle bedroom and talked at length with Jones, Glynn, Lucy Jones and nine-year-old Eileen. Pleasant working-class folk, they were anxious to avoid anything that might provoke a resumption of their sufferings. But they clearly held Davies in some regard and spoke candidly of the inexplicable happenings in the house. Jones told me that his wife had died some while earlier, of cancer. Lucy Jones said her husband had died in the front bedroom, the room in which she had been born.

Davies then drove to a farm on the outskirts of the town and introduced me to the residents, a man and wife. Two other visitors were also present, a woman and a local policeman. After some general conversation, our host beckoned me into another room and closed the door carefully behind us. Having asked for, and received, my promise that, until given permission to do so, I would reveal nothing of what he was about to disclose, he told an astounding story.

It appeared that Jones, the householder at Byron Street, had been employed as a part-time worker at the farm. Among other duties, he had assisted in caring for fifty-three pedigree pigs. A week before the Byron Street outbreak began, one of the beasts had died. Thought to be due to one of the problems associated with the raising of such animals, the event was given no particular significance. But, within a few days, several more were found dead. A veterinary surgeon was called. After careful examination of the carcases, he said he could find no reason for the deaths. There were, however, clear signs that the remaining animals were very nervous and frightened. Some fought each other. In one sty a terrified pig was seen trying to climb a wall as if to escape. Within a fortnight all fifty-three were dead, adding a large financial loss to their owner's bafflement. Five veterinary experts were engaged on inquiries. They examined the corpses and sent organs away for tests. The deaths remained a mystery.

Two days after the demise of his last pig, the farmer told me, he was amazed to see 'a black cloud' moving about his yard. He described it as 'about seven feet in height and shapeless except for two prongs sticking out at the back'. While he watched, it moved towards him, stopping four or five feet away. When he approached, it moved to his left, went in the direction of the empty pig-sties, entered an outhouse and disappeared. A quietly spoken, unemotional person, he admitted that his first reaction had been to doubt his own sanity. After reflection, he had decided to keep the incident to himself.

Forty-eight hours later, his wife told him she had seen a strange dark cloud moving about in the yard. Her description of the thing tallied with what he had seen himself. He then told her of his experience. They had stared at each other, mystified and unnerved.

For a few days nothing untoward occurred. Then, one night, a cow was heard bellowing with alarm. It was found in a state of great agitation, its eyes bulging and its entire body shivering with terror. For a long time it gave no milk.

Then the eerie 'cloud' was seen in the farmhouse kitchen. My informant said that, determined to find out what it was, he had brushed past it to switch on the light. As he did so, the two projecting prongs touched him on the side of his throat. They had felt 'solid, like two blunt sticks'. When the light went on, the phantom disappeared.

On a number of occasions unaccountable scratchings were heard in the drawers of a desk. Sometimes these sounds were followed by loud rattlings of the drawers. Once, jampots were inexplicably turned over in the larder.

It was during these events that the phenomena at Byron Street had reached their crescendo. Continuing to report for work at the farm,

Jones, distressed by lack of sleep, frayed nerves and bewilderment, begged his employer to visit his home, to see if anything could be done. At first, mindful of – but still silent about – the awesome mysteries on his own premises and giving priority to safeguarding his nine-year-old son, the farmer had refused to become involved. But, seeing that Jones' dismay was nearing a crisis, he finally allowed himself to be persuaded.

To his horror, one of the first inexplicable sights that had met his eyes in the 'haunted' bedroom was a black, two-pronged 'cloud' identical to the one encountered at the farm. It was on the large bed, which was then occupied by Glynn and Bury. 'I saw it clearly in the light of my torch,' he told me, 'but then it faded away.'

He had been wearing an overcoat on arrival at the house. In the bedroom, he removed and folded it and placed it on the dressing-table. As soon as the light was extinguished the coat was thrown over his head, enveloping the upper part of his body. This process was repeated three times in quick succession.

After a short period of silence in the darkness he had heard a slight noise and instantly switched on his torch. In its beam he had seen a book travelling horizontally across the room. In the midst of its flight it stopped suddenly, then fell straight down to the floor. Within moments it was followed by a second book, this time a Bible, which also stopped in mid-air, opened and scattered some loose pages before it too dropped to the floor.

His most alarming experiences at Byron Street had, he said, occurred when he was sitting on the small bed. Glynn's mother was seated beside him and the two Johns were occupying the large bed. All at once the pillows were whipped from under the boys' heads and flung across the room. The bedclothes were pulled off and Glynn was thrown across the two beds, his head on the double bed and his legs on the other. At the same time a chest standing near the single bed was moved diagonally across a corner of the room, forming a triangle. John Bury was then hurled into the triangular space, ending up jammed in with his arms and legs in the air. While this was going on, a sheet was wrapped round and round Mrs Glynn's head. All these movements had taken place simultaneously.

After various small articles had been flung about, my host told me, he had decided to address the destructive invader. 'If you can throw things, let's see if you can put them back again,' he called. To everyone's amazement, a drawer and two uprights from the semi-wrecked dressing table were immediately returned to their proper places.

Four months after he had first seen the strange 'cloud', he had gone out one morning to open a large shed in which a spaniel and sheepdog had spent the night. They rushed out with typical canine energy. Then, on turning to his left, he had seen the weird shape again loitering nearby. He noticed that it seemed smaller and lighter in shade. The dogs saw it too, for they dashed at it, barking and jumping up. Avoiding them, the 'cloud' moved away, rose into the air and vanished. It had not been seen since.

The man's sincerity and careful avoidance of overstatement were apparent. Now that life had returned to normal, he made light of the fact that nervous anxiety and tension at the height of the violent and costly oddities had caused him to be confined to bed under medical supervision.

His story completed, he called his wife into the room. I questioned her closely. Her main concern, she said, was that our conversation should be treated in strict confidence. She and her husband enjoyed some social standing in the locality and she dreaded the thought that their home might be subjected to invasion by ignorant and inconsiderate crowds of the kind that had swarmed into Byron Street. I promised that I would respect her wish and she gave me her account of what had occurred. It confirmed much of what her husband had told me, with one or two interesting additions.

She said that a few days before the death of the first pig, when everything appeared normal, she had made a long-distance telephone call from the farm. While waiting for connection she had suddenly seen an apparition of her husband's deceased father standing just a few feet away. He was dressed as he had appeared in life and was wearing his spectacles and smoking a cigarette. She remembered particularly noticing the long, drooping ash on the cigarette, which had been characteristic of his manner of smoking. At that moment her call had been put through and, as soon as she spoke, the wraith had melted away. She had seen the same figure on two subsequent occasions, once just outside one of the pig-sties after the deaths of the pigs.

Her description of the mysterious 'cloud' included the observation that the spectre had been opaque – it had obscured objects behind it. As it moved along she had seen that bits of paper and dust were swirled about as though caught up in a small whirlwind. She had noticed the two prongs protruding from the back. On one occasion she had watched, horrified, while it followed Jones as he left the farm. Something had stopped her from shouting a warning and he had not turned round or become aware of his pursuer.

Calm and dignified, she took some pains to impress upon me that neither she nor her husband had the slightest knowledge of, or interest in, Spiritualism. Like him, she had been chiefly concerned about protecting their young son. Showing me over the farm, the couple pointed out the various places where they had sighted the 'cloud'.

Davies drove to his home at Kingsley, where we dined with his wife and two women friends. Inevitably, the conversation revolved around hauntings and occultism. When the women's husbands arrived, well refreshed after a meeting of their masonic lodge, the ladies insisted on having a 'seance' with a wine-glass ouija board. By that time the atmosphere was more liquidly than ethereally spiritual and the result was nonsense. Departing, one of the females announced that she intended to 'play with the damn thing every night' in future because she felt certain there were scores of dead people waiting to talk to her.

Davies and I sat talking and theorizing about poltergeists until 2 a.m. It was the first of several hospitable nights he and Joan provided to me at Kingsley and in their next home at Hale Wood, near Liverpool. His enthusiasm for psychical research matched his kindness. Boyishly ebullient, he was tireless in discussing the classic cases of the past as well as his own remarkable experiences at Byron Street. He told me that, had he lived in the area, he would almost certainly have bought the remains of Borley Rectory when they were put on the market.

At my request he wrote and signed a statement describing what he had seen of the Runcorn infestation, giving his opinion on specific aspects and the individuals involved with them. He added his permission for my use of the document in any way I might wish. The following is an extract:

> I attempt, of course, no explanation of the cause, but I feel absolutely convinced that in some way the boy John Glynn was a prerequisite to the phenomena, either as a generative, receptive or amplifying factor. He is, as I told you, mentally and physically developed but in some mysterious way, to me at least, immature psychologically, and this seems to me – without knowing quite why – very significant and important. I do not feel at all that the strange happenings were due to any ghostly causation. But I might be very wrong. I feel certain that the cause lies somewhere in the boy's subconscious.
>
> The first night I visited the house I met, amongst others, the Revs Stafford of Runcorn, Stevens of Widnes and Lester of Widnes, all of the Methodist persuasion, two pressmen, the farmer and the family

concerned. The boy (John Glynn) had gone to bed together with his friend John Bury and grandfather Sam Jones, the two boys occupying the large bed and the grandfather the small. After some time a great noise as of banging furniture commenced, at which the people forgathered in the kitchen made their way upstairs and stood about or sat on the small bed. The lights were extinguished and after a short time, in the direction of the dressing-table of, I think, early Edwardian type, a great rumpus and noise started, as if it were being thrown against the wall. As this was near to the large bed, the possibility that the dresser was being pushed violently by the boy or boys did not escape me, but there was absolutely no preliminary sound of movement of the clothes as one might reasonably have expected.

At a prearranged signal by touch, the Rev Lester, who had his elbow on the electric light switch, the lights – at least 100 watts and three powerful torches – were switched on simultaneously. To my great astonishment, the dresser continued in full light to beat itself against the wall, rocking violently. This I imagine continued for about three seconds at least and certainly there was no possibility of physical contact from the bed.

After some time the boy John Glynn wished to urinate – a phenomenon which was much in evidence subsequently, surely proving a very tense and strained emotional state. The company went downstairs with him and partook of refreshment in the form of tea kindly provided by Mrs Lucy Jones, the housekeeper.

I, however, entirely alone, stayed behind lying on the bed in the approximate position of John Bury and attempted to move the dressing-table from a lying position, with my hand. [Davies weighed approximately 15 stones.] Although, with effort, I could do this I was not able to simulate at all the previous movement, which was extremely rapid.

I then tried to turn this furniture with my foot – stockinged feet – but this was quite impossible. The weight of the piece with all the drawers full I would estimate at approximately 1½ to two hundredweight. This itself almost convinced me that there was some force at work which could not possibly have been supplied by either or both of the youths in bed.

On the return to the bedroom of the boys and observers, many more strange things took place. Books and torches, a clock, ornaments, pillows etc in the darkness commenced to fly about. But it is certain that there was no preliminary sound of movement from the bed itself. I have excellent hearing and am quite certain of this.

On this and subsequent nights, many people were hit by one or other of the objects mentioned and it is a fact that if these missiles hit people no serious hurt was done. Often, however, these objects hit walls or doors, and great scars were afterwards visible, in some cases penetrating plaster to the brickwork.

> A curious smell was much in evidence to me on each visit, but not to everyone, and a sensation of coldness from the waist downwards, also some eye irritation. The odour may have been due to camphor in the drawers, but I do not think so. The sensation of coldness may have been due to physiological reactions, although there was no conscious feeling of apprehension in my case. Two thermometers which I placed at approximately the same height on opposite sides of the room showed no appreciable difference, and certainly there was no violent fluctuation in temperature on either thermometer.
>
> On another visit to the house, again at a pre-arranged signal, the lights were suddenly switched on, and I distinctly saw in excellent light a cardboard box almost in suspension above the bed. The behaviour of this box was not that of an ordinary trajectory, but almost as if it were being carried with directional intent. It hit a lady sitting on the small bed, who became hysterical.
>
> Being very interested, I took on two occasions a friend who is a most excellent photographer. On both these occasions nothing at all happened while we were there. I understand that afterwards on both occasions there was an outbreak of activity immediately we left. I feel that this may be significant.
>
> I visited the house on my way to business one morning about ten o'clock and was met at the door by Mrs Lucy Jones, who was in a state of great anxiety and was obviously ill with the strain. Inside, I was shown the bedroom and stairs. It appeared that the previous night all the furniture in the bedroom had been overturned, pillows ripped up and feathers were very much in evidence on the stairs and in the bedroom.
>
> The last occasion on which I visited the house as an observer was to spend the night in the room, undressed and in bed. Several times I got the impression that the bed was lifting, but as I had a very bad cold this may have been due to slight fever.

I kept in touch with Glynn for several years. After a brief spell in the army – he was eventually discharged on medical grounds – he settled back into civilian life and took an untroubled place among the ordinary people of our workaday world.

12. Gilbert Harding and *What's My Line?*

Even ghost-hunting has to have its lighter moments. It was on 12 April 1953 that I 'beat the panel' on the popular Sunday evening BBC Television game *What's My Line?* The occasion included an encounter with irascible 'TV personality' Gilbert Harding that made headlines and led to our friendship.

The suggestion that I should be a contestant having been made, I had a preliminary meeting with producer Leslie Jackson. Instructed to arrive at the Lime Grove, West London, studios – the present Wood Lane centre did not then exist – two hours before the programme was due to go on the air at 8 p.m., I found myself in the company of a small group of people whose 'lines' or occupations were as varied and improbable as the resourceful Jackson could find. One, a soap polisher named Josie Byrne, bore a striking resemblance to the Queen. We were instructed in the techniques of entrance, 'signing in' on a blackboard, presenting a short piece of mime characterizing our 'lines' and responding to panel-members' questions, by Irish ex-boxer, 'Question Master' Eamonn Andrews. Friendly towards the other contestants, he seemed to regard me rather warily. Rehearsal completed, we were turned loose in the canteen to fortify ourselves – non-alcoholically – for the contest.

By coincidence Lord Dowding, architect of victory in the Battle of Britain, with whom I had several times discussed his views on the paranormal, was the 'celebrity challenger' two weeks later. But the questions from the panellists, who were blindfolded before Dowding appeared, gave him no opportunity to speak of his Spiritualistic beliefs. Through interrogation that gradually centred on his military career, he was identified by Gilbert Harding. The celebrity on the programme in which I appeared was Walt Disney.

When my turn arrived, about halfway through the show, I met the examiners – actress Elizabeth Allan, Ghislaine Alexander, a member of a newspaper-owning family, 'comedian's straight-man' Jerry Desmonde and the spiky Gilbert. For my mime I pretended to be observing something of interest and making notes.

Questions were put by the panellists in turn. Elizabeth asked whether what I did was concerned with the living or the dead. I answered 'Both.' Ghislaine asked whether there was any connection with bones. I said there could be. Harding thought I might be a faith healer. Desmonde asked whether I was a Spiritualist. I said I wasn't. Elizabeth wanted to know whether my 'line' was unusual. I said it was a little so, at which Andrews cut in, 'That is a gross understatement.' After my tenth 'no', he presented me with a piece of rolled-up paper representing the certificate signed by himself, the panellists and producer that was sent to me later.

When Andrews asked me to reveal my 'line', I said that I was a psychical investigator, described for the purpose of the game as a 'ghost-hunter'. Harding's face turned purple, his eyes goggling behind his glasses. 'Do you really believe in ghosts?' he demanded. Not wanting to complicate my answer with qualifications, I said I did. 'You must be barmy!' he exploded. This, as he well knew it would, was the exclamation that produced the headlines next day.

There was uproar in the studio. Elizabeth whacked Harding's knuckles with her pencil. 'You mustn't insult a guest like that,' she cried. I whipped mentally through a choice of possible ripostes, recalling Harding's comments, in his column for the *People* newspaper that very day, about the death of Professor Joad. 'We say that Joad is dead,' he had written, 'but as he himself would say, "It depends what you mean by death." And those who read his last book, *The Recovery of Belief*, will know that, in fact, his spirit still lives.' Should I ask him how he differentiated between spirits and ghosts? Or, in view of his reputation for intemperate outbursts, should I simply inquire whether he spoke as an expert on good taste? The problem was removed when Andrews asked whether I could show them 'anything resembling a ghost'. By pre-arrangement, I had brought a tracing of one of the strange (and then unchallenged) wall-writings from Borley Rectory. It was flashed on the screen. It had, I explained, been deciphered as 'Well Tank Bottom Me' and had prompted Harry Price's brief excavation in the rectory cellar which resulted in the finding of part of a human female skull.

After the show, Harding stumbled towards me over the cables and muddle behind the set, hand extended. 'I apologize most humbly for my extreme rudeness,' he said. 'I hope I did not cause you too much offence. Of course I know that, as Shakespeare put it, "There are more things in heaven and earth than are dreamt of in our philosophy." ' I congratulated him on his instinct for publicity. There was no time then for a further exchange of views – I was called away to deal with telephone calls from journalists who were eager to include the comments of the 'insulted ghost-hunter' in their stories of Mount Harding's latest eruption.

The Press calls went on after I reached home, including visits by photographers who were sent to secure pictures of the fellow who had told eight million viewers that he believed there were such things as ghosts. Most of the newsmen wanted to know how I felt about being called 'barmy'. I said that everyone was entitled to a point of view and recounted a story I had been told at dinner with the Methodist crusader Donald (later Lord) Soper concerning a man who had propounded an unpopular theory in the course of a talk and was challenged by a member of his audience who had yelled the same message Harding had addressed to me. A quicker thinker than I am, the lecturer had instantly decided that his best course of defence was attack. 'Well, sir,' he responded, 'you may be right. I have no way of proving that I am sane. But, equally, neither have you.' 'Oh yes I have,' bawled his critic – and produced a certificate of discharge from a lunatic asylum!

'Ghost Hunter "Barmy" Says Mr Harding' and 'TV Panel Beaten' were the headlines over *Daily Telegraph* broadcasting correspondent L. Marsland Gander's story the following day. 'Knuckle-Rap for "Barmy" Remark' and 'Harding Apologises to Ghost-Hunter' appeared above a *News Chronicle* account by Norah Bowes. 'Harding: "You're Barmy," ' said the *Daily Express*. 'Gilbert Gets Knuckles Rapped,' said the *Daily Mirror*. 'You Must Be Barmy, Says Harding,' reported the *Daily Mail*. 'He Got A Rap,' said the *Daily Sketch*. Similarly headed stories appeared in the *Birmingham Post, Yorkshire Observer, Northern Echo, Nottingham Guardian* and other papers. Perhaps the classic headline among them all was that of the *Liverpool Daily Post*: 'Mr Harding Is Unkind Again.'

Some cartoonists joined in too. The London *Star* featured a drawing showing a ghost queuing for a telephone, anxious to tell Harding a thing or two. My favourite was a sketch by 'Artie' in the *Daily Express*. It showed two spectral figures standing in front of a television set, one asking the other 'Do you really believe in Gilbert Harding?' In the *Sunday Graphic*, 'Flip' depicted a man showing his friend two pictures hanging on a wall. The caption read: 'That's me when I appeared in *What's My Line?* and there's the handsome apology I received from Gilbert Harding.'

The *Sunday Graphic* asked if I was willing to take Harding on an all-night vigil in a 'haunted' house. I said I was. They invited him to join the venture. He refused. They challenged him about his contradictory stance concerning Joad, and I wrote to him on the subject. He responded in his *People* column:

> It is perfectly true that I apologised to Mr Philip Paul for a rather impolite remark to him on the TV *What's My Line?* programme last Sunday. But I still do not believe in ghosts.
>
> Since our encounter Mr Paul thinks he has caught me out. He asks me how I reconcile my remark in this column last Sunday about the survival of Cyril Joad's spirit with my scepticism about ghosts.
>
> The answer is perfectly simple. Of course I believe in spirits and survival after death. But I do not believe that people who are dead can be seen and talked to.

Faced with his rejection of their idea that he should join me for a night's ghost-hunting, the *Sunday Graphic* asked me to contribute an 'open letter' to him for their columns. It appeared on the same day as his explanation of his views in the *People*. Under portraits of my accuser and myself, with the headline 'You Called Me Barmy, Mr Harding', I wrote:

> ... by your round condemnation of a ghost-hunter last Sunday you 'certified' no fewer than 8,300,000 people in Britain. According to a recent survey of British religious life, that is the number of people who believe in ghosts. And no fewer than 3,500,000 say they have seen or heard a ghost ...
>
> I'm not claiming that every knock is a ghostly sign ... All too often one runs to earth 'ghosts' of disappointingly material origin. But buried amid the mass of the dubious, there is an unshakable hard core ... And in this conviction I'm in good company. Would you have described Sir Oliver Lodge as 'barmy'? Or Sir Arthur Conan Doyle? Or Sir William Crookes, Baron von Shrenck Notzing, Charles Richet?
>
> You seem to forget the clergy. ... What about the efforts they have made to quiet the ever-present poltergeist? Are the well-meaning exorcists 'barmy' too? Why did the Rev Francis Gripper bless every room in Tonbridge School in an endeavour to rid the building of an 'evil spirit'? Why did Canon F. Tucker try to exorcise the poltergeist which haunts the 18th century home of the Wilson family in Ipswich?

The same day the *Sunday Chronicle* published an item headed 'That's Life' by 'Dr Psycho':

> You must be barmy. Gilbert Harding, in making that comment to someone who had said he believed in ghosts, stirred up thousands of British homes.
>
> Fairy tales have bequeathed to each of us a fear of the supernatural. Walking down a country lane is an eerie business when the night is stormy, with black clouds scurrying across the moonlit sky. And what about that hesitating movement we heard as we sat alone by the fireside in an old house – just a mouse? The British are said to be the most ghost-minded people in the world. Perhaps because of our long winter evenings and boisterous weather. In Scotland, St Andrews, though a comparatively small place, has no fewer than 80 recorded ghosts ....

I was interviewed for the *Aberdeen Evening Express* by a talented journalist named Peter Chambers, who was later to become a star writer for the *Daily Express*. Among his subsequent exploits, he spent a night in the Tussaud waxworks 'chamber of horrors'. Of our meeting, he wrote:

> My lunch with a ghosthunter was no psychic phenomenon. It was solid. We had soup, chicken, fruit salad and drinks. 'The ghosts don't follow you around,' I said. 'I was hoping a poltergeist would throw a stone in my beer.'
>
> 'You're a sceptic,' replied Philip Paul. 'Like Gilbert Harding this week – he said I was barmy.' I denied I thought he was barmy. I was keeping an open mind. I'd just never seen a ghost, that's all ...
>
> What about the faked-up manifestations with muslin drapery and a broomstick? 'There are thousands of frauds,' agreed Paul. ... 'But there remains the hard core of inexplicable happenings.'
>
> Paul has investigated haunted houses as far apart as Edinburgh and Spain ... . Poltergeists are mischievous, fickle. They don't work to schedule.
>
> I'm still not sure about ghosts, but Paul seemed a genuine character to me. He was frank about fakes. 'You know, there are people,' he said, 'who fix poltergeist phenomena just to get rid of their mother-in-law.'

The Spiritualist Press joined in. Wrote Maurice Barbanell, editor of *Two Worlds*, in a leading article headed 'Harding is on the Spot':

> Skilful performer though he is, Gilbert Harding has impaled himself on the horns of a dilemma. After dismissing as 'barmy' people who believe in ghosts, he said he believed in spirits. Furthermore, he believes in survival after death, but rejects the idea that people who are dead can be seen and talked to.

Harding makes a distinction between ghosts and spirits that is not supported by dictionaries. For example, *Nuttall's Standard Dictionary* defines a ghost as 'the soul of a deceased person; the soul or spirit separate from the body.' Its definition of a spirit is 'a spiritual being; the soul; a disembodied soul or ghost.'

That makes nonsense of Harding's assertion that he believes in spirits but not ghosts. Harding might say that he thinks of ghosts in terms of phantoms with clanking chains and regards spirits as the essence of individuality that persists. If, however, he studied the subject, which obviously he has not, he would know that ghosts are earthbound spirits.

The views of Gilbert Harding do not matter so much, except that his rude interjection has been the means of bringing valuable publicity to the subject which he tried to pooh-pooh. The fact that scores of newspapers regarded his outbursts against ghosts as news is a tribute to the interest of the man in the street – his outbursts in themselves are surely not news.

The Gilbert Hardings are the anachronisms and very much in the minority. The truth is that he has not even got a ghost of a case.

A *Psychic News* leader headed 'When Opportunity Knocks' read:

P.T. Barnum, the great showman, had an axiom that all publicity was good publicity. Let us consider in this connection the experience of Philip Paul. Because he believed in ghosts he was abused by Gilbert Harding in a recent television programme.

But Paul's was the claim of a rational observer who had based his beliefs on solid evidence. After the Harding gibe he was permitted a few minutes to make this point.

Next day the national newspapers made quite a splash with the story and at least one devoted space to Paul's researches at Borley. And last week-end the *Sunday Graphic* gave the ghosthunter a full page in which he replied to Gilbert Harding.

So, not in spite of, but because of Harding's adverse comment, Paul's views reached a wider public than he could have hoped when he made his appearance on TV.

Psychic Realm, a new journal in the field launched by a former *Two Worlds* editor named Ernest Thompson, declared that I was to be congratulated for not letting Harding get away with his attack.

Barbanell took me up on my remark to Chambers about 'poltergeist phenomena' having been 'rigged' for the purpose of removing an unwanted mother-in-law. Was I joking? he asked in an editorial item. I replied in doggerel, which he published:

It was no joke re mother-in-law,
(a social problem, very sore).
Authenticated case was quoted –
poor 'poltergeist', so soon demoted!

Harding's affairs prospered in step with his ability to keep himself contentiously in the public eye. In addition to his broadcasting and journalistic activities he accepted numerous private engagements, at some of which he got himself into clashes with his hosts. In one case, he was sued, and forced to pay damages, for his blunt remarks at a civic luncheon.

He was also engaged to write a regular column for the Hulton weekly magazine *Picture Post*. Towards the end of November 1953 he wrote to me:

> Although it is Advent, but because we are working for a magazine which 'goes to bed' (if you will pardon the expression) so early, we must give our Christmas Party in anticipation of The Birthday.
>
> Will you please come to 96 Piccadilly on Saturday December 5, between 9 p.m. and midnight, to be greeted, thanked and refreshed (and possibly photographed). Mr Edward Hulton also hopes that you will come.

He was in benevolent mood at the party. Resplendent in a silk polka-dot waistcoat and sporting a white carnation in the buttonhole of his jacket, he put an arm round my shoulder while we were photographed. The picture that appeared in the Christmas issue of *Picture Post* was captioned: 'No hard feelings between ghosthunter Philip Paul and me. I once told him "You must be barmy" in *What's My Line?* But that was before we met properly.'

His other guests included two up-and-coming young comedians named Norman Wisdom and Frankie Howerd, BBC executive Ronnie Waldman (best known for his pre-war radio programme *Monday Night at Eight*) and his actress wife Lana Morris, TV programme presenter Noëlle Middleton, drama critic Kenneth Tynan and his actress wife Elaine Dundy, scriptwriter Alfred Shaughnessy and a stunningly beautiful newcomer to the small screen, Katie Boyle. Champagne and conversation flowed freely. I was called upon to tell a light-hearted Christmas ghost story.

Writing of the party afterwards, Harding commented: 'This was a very happy evening. We just had fun and games, and sundry conversation, with no time for harsh criticism, rancour, back-biting or complaint.' There was no mention of his physical sufferings that night. He was in the grip of the heart and lung ailments that were to kill him. He interrupted a conversation I was having with Elaine Dundy to ask me to accompany him outside. With him leaning on my shoulder and panting for breath, we went to the entrance steps and stood for a while gazing at the passing traffic. Gradually his breathing eased and his face took on a softer hue.

He turned to me confidingly. 'I need your advice,' he said. He told me that on a number of recent occasions when he had been alone, he had heard, unmistakably, the voice of his sister and former flatmate Constance, who had died from cancer. What did I make of it? Was he going mad or was there some other explanation? He was plainly disturbed and upset; this, I saw, was the real, susceptible person who lived hidden behind the raucous and tormented shell that had given him fame.

I told him that I too had had a sister whose second name was Constance and recounted the strange occurrence that had coincided with her death. He listened attentively and seemed comforted. Lighting a cigarette, he remarked that we must all die sooner or later. He was not afraid of death but only of the business of dying. And when his time came, he had no doubt some publicity-seeking crank would claim that he had communicated from the other world, expressing contrition for his bad behaviour on earth.

He might reasonably have been as much concerned about 'mystic' readings during his lifetime as troubled by thoughts of any occurring after his death. Launching a series of articles on 'BBC Hands' in an occult magazine in January 1955, a palmist wrote of him: 'We see that the Life Lines are long and widely curved – indicative of good vital force. Ahead into the foreseeable future there are shown continuing material success and stability, personal satisfaction and happiness and also, almost certainly, enrolment on the list of honours in the not-distant future.' Harding received no honours, was certainly not happy, was only precariously alive rather than charged with 'good vital force' and at the time of the article had less than six years to live.

He died, aged fifty-three, on the steps of a BBC studio in Portland Place, after taking part in a recording of the radio programme *Round Britain Quiz*, on 16 November 1960. His end was almost instantaneous – just as he would have wished; he was not called upon to endure much of 'the business of dying'.

The story of his death, carried by every national newspaper the following day, coincided with the news that eighty-five-year-old Sir

Winston Churchill had broken a bone in his spine.

Four months later it was revealed that Harding had left £27,000, bequeathing most of it to the man who had been his long-suffering secretary for eight tempestuous years, thirty-five-year-old Roger Storey. In his moving and tenderly written book *Gilbert Harding*, published in 1961, Storey told of his wearing but rewarding life in the service of an employer who could one moment be a beaming delight and the next a bellowing tyrant. I am glad that, among his recollections, he thought it worth mentioning my friendship with the lonely and frightened man who concealed his poignant psyche behind a mask of belligerent bombast.

13. Revival of the Ghost Club

As Spiritualists are commonly accused of credulity, what similar generalization might be applied to those who range under the divergent, though related, banners of 'organized' psychical research?

Besmirched by bitter feuds and rivalries, the annals speak for themselves. Fuelled by deceit, prejudice, spite, ego-inflation and lust for publicity, the antagonisms sometimes soil the aggressors as badly as their targets. Death, with its removal of the protection afforded by the laws restraining libel and slander, is the signal for onslaughts on envied reputations. Perhaps the most saddening reflection of all is that the human mind should fail to be expanded, in scope or generosity, by application to the most profound mysteries of life.

I should have remembered these facts when, in 1953, I set about resuscitating the Ghost Club, a body of socially minded inquirers founded in 1862, recreated by Harry Price and made defunct by his death in 1948. I was swiftly reminded of them. Still possessing all my files, I can recount the events with precision.

Against my better judgement, I had taken on unpaid editorial duties for a hobby-horse psychical research association run by a retired businessman named Percival Seward. For two years I struggled with his voluminous correspondence, committee meetings and other demands. Eager to get the Ghost Club restarted, I sought his support. We discussed the proposal with the club's former vice-chairman, K.E. Shelley QC, at his Temple, London, chambers in December 1953. His reactions were positive and an interim committee was formed. In February 1954 we sent a circular to 452 former members, asking whether they favoured a restart of the club at an annual subscription of 10 shillings and with dinners at 23s/6d a head.

The replies totalled 167, 126 supporting revival. There were over a hundred suggestions as to how the reformed club should be run, ranging from 'There should be a panel of members to help in investigations of interesting psychical occurrences' to 'Make it clear it is for social and entertainment purposes only; there are more than enough Societies for Psychical Research already.' There were also some tributes. One, dated 16 February 1954, was addressed to me by a publisher's assistant named Peter Underwood. In it he told me 'You have been more successful than I; I tried very hard in 1949 to get Miss Wilkinson [the former secretary] to carry on with the club, but all to no avail.' He added 'I should very much like to be associated with the organization and running of the revived Ghost Club and hope you will do what you can to help me in this connection.'

The storm clouds were then gathering over the dead (and therefore defenceless) Price's work at Borley. Shelley warned me that a report was being prepared by three members of the Society for Psychical Research in an attempt to show that Price had faked 'phenomena'. When I told him of this, Seward became alarmed. In a long letter to me he wrote: 'In advocating revival of the Ghost Club we have ... nailed our flag to the HP mast and I would find it disconcerting to discover that we were sailing under the "Skull and Crossbones." I have spent some time in exploring possibilities of HP chicanery. I have been informed ... of some instances ... which I find irrefutable.' He added: 'I am at least convinced that you are thoroughly honest and equally so that HP was not. So good luck to you and to those *justified* iconoclasts who, in dethroning Investigator HP, unwittingly befriend Investigator PP.'

Further letters made it clear that he regarded those who were in favour of revival of the club with a similarly cynical eye. Among other things he wrote: 'The "assentors" number many testy and opinionated folk who would cause a lot of trouble if not ridden with a firm hand. I foresee an enormous amount of work, friction and general unpleasantness ... Were it not that I have made a bet with myself that I know how it can be done ... I would not bother any further. I am removing all ambiguity with regard to Mr Shelley by asking his intentions with regard to the presidency.'

Shelley told us that he would be willing to accept the presidency 'only if we cannot find someone with real publicity value for that post.' Acting on the nominations received, the interim committee elected him vice-president, Seward chairman and me vice-chairman and public relations officer. Society ear-piercer and restaurant owner Cyril Wilkinson, father of the club's former secretary, was also elected and catering contractor Leonard Kingston became treasurer. The presidency was left open, pending the finding of a suitably notable public personality. Two potential candidates we had in mind were Aldous Huxley and Sir Osbert Sitwell.

After several committee meetings I wrote to Underwood, on 14 July 1954, telling him that I had been able to propose him, successfully, for committee membership. A month later I sent him further information. Writing from a new address, he acknowledged it, and my earlier news, on 25 August. Explaining that his time had been taken up with his move of home, he commented 'I am very interested in all the plans for the Ghost Club. I shall be happy to do all I can as far as my commitments will allow.'

By this time the committee was well advanced with preparations for a re-inaugural dinner. But there was difficulty in finding an honorary secretary. I heard that the Psychosomatic Research Association, scene of some extraordinary parascientific proceedings, was closing and its secretary, a retired medical general practitioner named Christabel Nicholson, widow of a naval man, had time on her hands. Seward was frank over my proposal of her name. He wrote: 'I have no objection to your suggestion as a solution to our secretarial problem; we must have one and the devil you know ... She is an intelligent woman but I think her powers are on the wane. If she should introduce a decimal point of the muddle in her flat to the affairs of the GC, God help us. We must keep her blind spots in mind and handle her accordingly.'

Christabel leapt at the invitation. Sadly, I did not then know that she had been an admirer of the Hitler regime who had been detained under Britain's wartime Defence Regulations. That information reached me later. But she quickly made her attitude felt. In a letter she told me: 'We are carefully ruling out the Spiritualist element, also the frivolous. There was a semi-religious element in the Psychosomatic which militated against normal people going – when you get "healers" interested you flood the place with quacks. We can work quite comfortably with the SPR. They are cultivated and can spell! Probably they are quite right to be critical, but are also nauseated by mediums, as I am. We were entirely autocratic with our members – they found me difficult to get by, mainly because of my medical degrees. We used to put on glorious shows and find a crew of women in fur capes and mad-looking men sitting in front – most disappointing.'

Her views were rigorously implemented, causing upsets among would-be members. Receiving complaints about her conduct, I told Seward of my uneasiness. He wrote: 'She is not pliable and I have encountered few given to greater irresponsibility of statement.'

But the doctor would not be restrained. Eventually, a showdown became unavoidable. During a business visit to the area, I called for a talk with Seward at his home in Hove, Sussex. He said she must be removed from office and charged me with the task of recovering the club's records and correspondence from her. As chairman, he gave me a letter addressed to Christabel, asking her to surrender the papers. I drove to her Kensington flat, handed her Seward's note and asked for the paperwork. Fuming with rage, she refused to part with it.

Next day she sent me a long Express Delivery letter apologizing for her rudeness. The committee met. Again she was apologetic. We accepted her assurance that she would change her approach to the club's affairs. She didn't. To a message demanding that she be allowed to address the re-inaugural dinner she attached a press-clipping photograph of an unprepossessing-looking Spiritualist medium. On it she had scribbled 'I can get you thousands of members who look like this.'

Seward was aghast. He wrote to me: 'I rang her up to remind her that she had said she was prepared not to speak. She blew up. Her main refrain was that the secretary arranged these things in co-operation with the chairman and treasurer, which really meant that she did. I contemplate offering my resignation after the dinner if she does not vacate the secretaryship.'

The dinner, which was well attended, duly took place in a West End restaurant. We ate *consommé à l'innocent, filet de sole Portugaise, caneton rôtis* and *bombe glacé praliné*. Shelley explained the objectives behind the revival. Seward spoke at length about the policy of the resurrected club. I thanked everyone who had helped to turn my hopes into reality. Pointing out that the club was rightly being selective in the matter of electing a president, I said it was not inappropriate for such a body to be headless. Trying to inject a little light-heartedness into the atmosphere arising from the behind-the-scenes situation, I ended with a joke about a woman who had said she considered men more useful after death than during their lives. When asked why she held this view, she had replied 'Well, my husband didn't do a thing when he was alive, but he works all right now – I've got his ashes in an egg-timer!'

Then came the shocks.

Immediately after the dinner, Seward performed a staggering *volte-face*. In a note to committee members he referred to 'a serious disagreement, largely of a personal nature, between two members of the committee.' Making no mention of the views he had expressed earlier about Christabel's failings, his message added: 'I feel that any attempt to apportion blame would be futile.' He asked for comments 'which will enable me to decide whether or not to tender my resignation.' In a covering letter to me he wrote 'Members' opinions which have come to my ears do not persuade me that the dinner was much of a success.'

I attended the next meeting of the committee, at the time I had been given. When I arrived the proceedings were already in progress. The first item on the written agenda was: 'To confirm that the secretary should be a voting member of the committee.' Christabel was so empowered. Other matters were disposed of with similar alacrity. Seward and Christabel laughed and joked together. I handed over a number of letters I had received from people seeking membership of the club and, leaving the engrossed party drinking tea, departed.

Two weeks later, Christabel sent out an announcement that an illustrated lecture was to be given by seance photographer Leon Isaacs. The note began 'A most successful re-inaugural dinner was … attended by a representative gathering of over 100 enthusiastic members and their guests … ' Was this, I wondered, the same 'not much of a success' occasion on which Seward had commented? I attended the Isaacs talk and, subsequently, one given by James Laver. Both were personal friends of mine.

Later, Seward wrote to me: 'I have consulted legal opinion regarding the status of club officers, having regard to the manner of their "election" last autumn. It seems that the method adopted was *ultra vires* and that the officers have no legal existence unless elected at a meeting of club members called, *inter alia*, for that purpose. At the forthcoming annual general meeting, it will be proposed that the present self-elected committee be elected as members of a council. The other "officers" feel that there should be no specified vice-chairman but that any member of the council should be eligible to function in that capacity, in which I concur.'

I replied, sending copies to all members of the committee:

> If, as you say, the proposal to abolish my office arises from the spontaneous demands of other committee members, I bow to their judgment … Since you raise the question of constitution, may I observe that, if the original election be ruled *ultra vires*, there has been a good

deal of *imperium in imperio* about subsequent proceedings. I had hoped there would come a time when we might all work together in a spirit of amity and co-operation. I feel it sad that we who evince an interest in a boundless subject should be narrow in our personal thinking. My ambition was to see the club resuscitated and I like to think I played some part in achieving that end. I should like to continue to be associated with it, but only if that may be in a spirit of friendliness and mutual respect. If that cannot be, I would rather we went our separate ways in a complete and final manner.

Seward answered: 'The members of the committee have considered your letter .... As, under the circumstances, you would "prefer we went our separate ways in a complete and final manner" – so be it.'

And so it was.

For me, the hurtful ending of my connection with the club was, to some extent, relieved by the renewed ability to pursue my interests in psychical research unencumbered by petty Machiavellianism. The episode also taught me a memorable lesson concerning human perfidy.

For anyone wondering why I should have troubled to recall this unhappy experience, my answer is that accurate reports whose veracity can be proven never harm the guiltless. Moreover, such records may, on occasion, aid identification of the distortions that sometimes gain currency when the evidence of truth is presumed to have vanished.

I am glad that others enjoyed the revival I was able to initiate.

14. Evil Picture?

Can inanimate objects exert malevolent powers? For most of us the question is simply a joke. For a tortured few the answer is anything but humorous.

Usually people of extreme sensitivity, they are sometimes compulsive ritualists – individuals who have become convinced that failure to perform specific acts will cause them to be visited by some terrible misfortune. This susceptibility takes many forms. One man I know, a commercial traveller, carries a pocket compass for the sole (an unintended pun) purpose of ensuring that he always places his shoes pointing north before going to bed. Another acquaintance, a woman, will never drink tea on Wednesdays and always turns her overcoats inside out when not wearing them.

Pause before you laugh. Many mental quirks have links with ancient superstitions. Have you never thrown a pinch of spilt salt over your shoulder? Never crossed your fingers as a symbol of hope? Never bought a gipsy's 'lucky' charm? Never avoided walking under a ladder? Never felt the least anxiety about Friday the 13th?

I have been consulted in several instances in which evil effects were said to be arising from everyday articles. One such was brought to me by middle-aged Mrs Dorothy Jenkins, of Clarendon Drive, Putney, South London. She told me she had been captivated by an old oil painting she saw in a Fulham junk shop. Signed 'Antoine', it showed the full-length figure of a doe-eyed young woman in a tight-waisted, square-necked, lace-frilled, red velvet gown. She wore a wedding ring and in her right hand held a closed fan. The four-feet-square canvas had been patched in several places and showed signs of scorching. Mrs Jenkins paid the tiny price asked and took her acquisition home.

Five years later, desperately seeking help, she said the picture had brought her a long series of troubles. But she was afraid to dispose of or destroy it; someone had persuaded her that to 'spurn' it would cause its unpleasant visitations to be increased to even more horrendous levels.

I visited Mrs Jenkins in her gloomy home. Grey-haired, pallid-faced and plainly under serious stress, she showed me the painting and introduced me to her son, who was in his thirties. She told me they had both suffered nervous breakdowns since she had brought the picture into the house.

At first, she had hung it in her bedroom. But she had grown uneasy with it, several times feeling that the eyes followed her as she moved about. Then it had been put in her son's room. Within a few months he had had a nervous collapse necessitating hospital treatment. His fiancée jilted him. Then came serious financial troubles. Pale, thin and agitated, he told me that all pleasure had gone from his life. His appetite had vanished; when he sat at table, he heard voices telling him not to eat. It was not a case of sheltered over-mothering. He had served in the Army, in tanks in Germany. He had been a good musician and singer, having received commendations for his vocal and organ performances in a neighbourhood church.

Mrs Jenkins told me their doctor had said that everything possible had been done for her son; was there anything further I could suggest? I promised to ask spiritual healer Harry Edwards to put him on his absent healing list, and did so.

As to the picture, I proposed that I should arrange a test with a suitable medium. Mrs Jenkins agreed at once. After some discussion, we decided that, to avoid any possibility of the sensitive being influenced by the dismal atmosphere of the house, the experiment would best be staged elsewhere. Mrs Jenkins said she had a friend living in nearby Fulham, where she felt sure appropriate arrangements could be made. I left her with detailed instructions as to preparation for the test, the basis being that she would hang a number of pictures of various sizes, including the 'evil' one, on the walls of a living-room.

The next step was to select a medium. I telephoned Ena Twigg. The only information I gave was that, while blindfolded, she would be required to psychometrise a number of objects somewhere in London. She accepted the challenge. Accompanied by a friend, Leslie Howard, who was then assistant editor of *Psychic News*, I met Ena and her husband Harry at Oxford Circus underground station and we drove to Fulham.

Some Press interest had been expressed and, since there was no case for secrecy, I had invited four newspaper people to be present – three reporters and a photographer. With Mrs Jenkins and her friend Mrs Violet Smith, they were awaiting our arrival in Fulham. No introductions were made. After warming herself briefly in front of a gas fire, Ena said she was ready. I blindfolded her securely and led her, for the first time, into the test room.

Reasoning that she would expect to be presented with an initial 'smokescreen', I took her straight to the 'sinister' picture and placed her hands on it. She recoiled in horror. 'There is great distress,' she said. 'There is a feeling of shaking all over. I am so afraid I may have to go away. I am alone. There is a danger I may do something. Things are going round and round. This house has got on top of me. I can't see properly. Things are very peculiar. I hear music. I want to call Mum, that is the only person I feel safe with. A lot of lights. I can see blood. Soldiers of the Queen. They have injected the truth drug. They won't even let me shave myself properly. You mustn't give up hope. They are talking about doing something with shocks.'

These remarks, most of them accurately reflecting the troubles experienced by Mrs Jenkins' son, who was not present, were the most emphatic of the evening. I conducted Ena – still blindfolded – to seven other pictures, putting her fingers on each in turn. She rinsed her hands in a bowl of water between each contact. There were no further violent reactions and only vague clairvoyant impressions until we came to the last one, which was the only photograph – of Mrs Jenkins' son. Touching it, Ena said: 'This doesn't feel like a picture. It is like one somebody has taken. I can feel blackness. It is all black. Is it my boy? Before and after. I have got to go on. I must fight to the last ditch and the last halfpenny I have got. I feel this is so sad. All my senses seem to be going.' The photograph, like most of the paintings, was in a glass-fronted frame. Ena did not touch the actual print.

I led her out of the room and removed the blindfold. During our absence, by previous arrangement, the positions of most of the pictures were changed, the 'mystery' painting being put on a wall opposite to its place during the test. Taking Ena back, I asked whether any particular picture attracted her attention. There were about twenty on the walls, but only eight had been used for the psychometry. After a pause she said she had seen a bright light flash from one side of the room to the other. Asked to explain, she said: 'It went from that one' – pointing to the 'suspect' painting – 'to that one' – pointing to a portrait of an elderly male, which had been put in the place formerly occupied by the 'sinister' picture.

I thought the test had been interesting, if only because of Ena's precise identifications of the two most significant items displayed. Not wishing to hurt her feelings, I made no comment on the fact that the information she had given provided no grounds on which ESP – thought transference – could have been eliminated as a possible source of her intelligence.

Reading her biography, *Ena Twigg, Medium*, I was amused to note that her recollections of the evening were not as accurate as might have been expected of a psychic. Of our rendezvous at Oxford Circus, the book says: 'Mr Paul insisted on blindfolding me. I must have looked a pretty picture being led through that crowded station blindfolded. Harry was dreadfully embarrassed.' After remarking that the blindfold was not removed until she entered the test room (in fact, it was only then that it was applied), her account describes the meeting with four journalists, a photographer and Mrs Jenkins and her friend as 'a room that was one seething mass of men with scribbling pads and pencils, the air blue with cigarette smoke – the worst possible conditions for a sensitive to work in'.

Her reactions during the experiment are recorded as follows: 'Not only had I picked out the correct picture, but I also began to re-enact the tragedy attached to it, although the story that came to me was so evil and frightening and personal that I hesitated to tell it to a large group of reporters. I ... began to relate the bare bones of the story. ... As I went on I knew that there was a great deal of evil here and that our hostess really did not want me to go on, so I respected her wishes and did not tell all. I suggested instead that she come to see me privately. She never did.'

Having some pride in the clarity of my memory – not to mention reliance on my shorthand notes – I believe it is fair to add that I have no record or remembrance of any derogatory comment being made by the press people. There was certainly none in their write-ups. But, according to Ena's life story, 'The reporters ... were not at all impressed with the accuracy of my performance ... For the most part they believed and said that "somebody must have tipped her off in advance." With some people, it wouldn't matter if you brought the sun, moon and stars down and put them in their proper rotation. They would still be doubters.'

Leaving Fulham that night, I was pleased to see that Mrs Jenkins looked less dejected. I advised her to dispose of the aggravating picture in whatever way she found easiest.

15. Some 'Ghosts' That Weren't

'They say their whatnot is haunted; would you have a look and let us know what you think?'

This was the request telephoned to me by the *Daily Mirror*. It sent me to a modest home above a little grocery store in Edmonton, North London.

The residents and shopkeepers were forty-three-year-old Richard Parsons and his wife Irene. They occupied the premises with their two daughters, sixteen-year-old Evelyn, a shorthand-typist, and ten-year-old schoolgirl Ann. Before acquiring the business, Parsons had served in the RAF, worked in an aircraft factory and been a London bus-driver. Disturbed by strange events that appeared to centre on the piece of furniture, Irene had written to the *Mirror* appealing for help.

Questioning elicited the fact that the couple had had some interest in Spiritualism, Irene being told she was psychic and her husband having experienced 'trance control' in a development circle. They said they had not continued their contact with the movement for fear that the subject might become an obsession.

The whatnot, a triangular structure of flimsy wood some six feet tall, two feet wide and ten inches deep, stood in a corner of the small living-room. I estimated its total weight as little more than ten pounds. Its three shelves were framed by lattices or ornamental carving, hand-worked, with machine-turned columns on either side. There were crudely executed inlays of mother-of-pearl. Its Moorish appearance was confirmed by Arabic characters carved in horizontal strips at the top and across the fronts of the shelves. These were later examined by R.H. Pinder-Wilson, a British Museum expert on oriental antiquities, and identified as verses from the Koran. I was told that the whatnot had been purchased, 'for a very small sum', some thirteen years earlier, from a Hungarian couple 'down on their luck' who had occupied part of a Tottenham, North London, house that was then the Parsons' home.

From the beginning, said Mrs Parsons, the whatnot had emitted strange knocks. They occurred at all hours but particularly during the evening and at night. Its movement into various rooms at their present and previous homes had made no difference to the sounds. The 'performance' did not seem to be affected by temperature, because the article had been kept in cold, as well as warm, places.

At their former address, Mrs Parsons told me, there had been two more pronounced incidents. On the first occasion, in the presence of five people one afternoon, a cream jar standing on the top shelf had suddenly 'exploded'. The jar had been replaced by a glass biscuit-barrel. Alone in the room some time later, Mrs Parsons said, she had heard a tinkle of glass. Looking towards the whatnot, she had seen the lid of the barrel rise about $1\frac{1}{2}$ inches from its place, remain suspended for a second or so, then drop back into a tilted position.

I examined the whatnot carefully. The rear panels were loose and rickety. The top, 'roof' section was without screws on one side and could be pushed up and down, making a loud creaking and knocking noise. I demonstrated to the Parsons that, with very little movement or vibration, the article produced strong sounds. To underline my point, I showed how the smallest floor or atmospheric tremor would suffice to cause these effects. They seemed to accept my explanation. At my suggestion they brought a screwdriver and some screws and I secured the loose parts. With the object restored to its corner, it was left that the Parsons would telephone me the moment they noticed any further 'odd' emissions.

The thing was evidently silenced; at all events, I heard nothing further of it – until, eight months later, a Sunday newspaper ran a 'seasonal Christmas ghost story' featuring a photograph of young Evelyn with the 'haunted' article and a recitation of all the 'unaccountable noises' it was said to have produced. The Parsons were reported to be spending Christmas shudderingly awaiting whatever new surprises the 'eerie' item might have in store.

How was ex-miner and Apostolic lay-preacher James Richards photographed seven days after his death and two days after burial in a tight-packed Rhondda graveyard?

This was the question with which I was confronted during a visit to South Wales. After giving a talk about Borley at a Spiritualists' summer school in Penarth, I was presented with the puzzle by the school's organizer, Mabel Hibbs, and her lively minded thirty-seven-year-old son Gordon. Mabel, an ardent Spiritualist, was convinced that the photograph was proof of Richards' survival. Gordon's view was that when the picture – intended to be of his grave – was taken by his daughter-in-law, the strong remembrance of the dead man which must have been in her mind might account for the result.

My first step was to visit the photographer and her husband, forty-five-year-old collieryman Ivor Richards, at their home at Heol Orchwy, Treorchy. Their accounts of how the 'miraculous' photograph was obtained were rendered in the musical accents of the area.

I heard that seventy-six-year-old James Richards, of Cwmparc, had died of a cerebral haemorrhage on 2 July and been buried on 7 July. On 9 July his daughter-in-law had borrowed a ready-loaded box camera from her neighbour and taken three snapshots of the freshly made-up grave. The camera had then been returned to its owner, who despatched the film to a developing and printing firm in Glasgow. When the pictures were returned, there were two views of the grave. The third shot showed an apparently recumbent, heavy-featured face crowned by wispy white hair against a totally black background – like the grim interior of a closed coffin.

'I was having a meal when they showed me the picture,' burly, square-jawed Ivor Richards told me. 'My stomach turned over. I can't think of any explanation, for no picture was taken of my father after death. But even if that had been done, there would still be something wrong, for my father's face was bandaged and the picture shows no bandage. Also, he was bald, whereas the picture shows what seems to be wispy hair. But it would be nonsense to say it is not my father when I go cold every time I look at it. Everyone who knew him recognizes the picture. Before he became a Christian fifty-five years ago, my father was a mountain fighter. He was lame because of a hip injury when he was a baby, but he was as strong as an ox. Once, he lifted a coping stone from a bridge and dropped it near two policemen standing underneath.

'He had a nose like the thumb of a boxing glove. There it is in the picture. Yet I have never known my father to smoke or drink or raise his hand to me. Even when we were at work I would never dare to open my box before he opened his and gave thanks for the meal of food. We showed the picture to the minister of the Apostolic church, but he only offered to destroy it for us. It seems almost as though the camera penetrated the earth and the coffin and photographed my father's face underground. Yet I know such a thing could not happen.' He added that a local Spiritualist had told him the photograph was a sign from his father that he should give up drinking.

In pouring rain, I went to Treorchy's steeply sloping hillside cemetery and took my own photographs of James Richards' resting place. As I wandered among the sodden graves, I saw a human head bobbing just above the ground. A man was opening a family grave in preparation for a burial the following day. We chatted awhile as his spade scraped nearer the lid of a long-buried coffin.

News of the 'miracle' photograph had spread like wildfire in the district. The gravedigger had heard of it and somehow guessed that it was connected with my visit. 'This is certainly the place for thinking,' he said, his gumboots splashing in the water that accumulated as he dug. Stooping to brush earth from a corroded brass nameplate, he added: 'The dead can speak for themselves, you know.' I raised my eyebrows questioningly. 'Listen,' he said and, grinning, swept the spade in an arc above his head, embedding the edge of the blade in the rotting coffin-lid on which he was standing. Great bubbles of released gas gurgled noisily up through the muddy water. 'There you are,' he chortled.

Back in London, I went into the photographic technicalities. It was then that I found the key to the problem. Mrs Richards' photographs had been taken on a type of film producing paper instead of the more usual transparent celluloid negatives. Because of the poor focus of the 'miracle' picture, no print had been made of it and the negatives had been returned with the other, paper, prints. The recognition of James Richards in the snapshot had, therefore been based on a reversal of normal light and dark areas. What appeared to be the murky inside of a coffin had really been light – in fact, the sky. And what had seemed to be wispy white hair was, in reality, dark.

With some difficulty, I obtained a print from the negative. It was at once apparent that the face was female. After a little more study it became obvious that it was a photograph of Mrs Richards, taken from chest level and looking directly upwards under her chin. With the assumption that the picture had been taken from the normal angle, the illusion was created of the face of someone lying horizontal, as in death.

Somehow, it seemed, Mrs Richards had unwittingly photographed herself when she thought she was snapping her father-in-law's grave.

But how had this happened? At first I thought that she must have unknowingly released the shutter while the lens was upturned towards her face, but the weakness of the theory was that, had such a mishap occurred, she would not have wound the film onwards and the subsequent snap taken with the simple camera would have produced a double exposure. With all its imperfections, the picture was obviously a single exposure.

The final link in the puzzle was found by inspecting the camera. A cheap reflex type, it employed two lenses, the second mounted above the picture-taking lens as part of the viewfinder. Gordon Hibbs discovered the last piece of the jigsaw. Holding the camera to his chest with the picture-taking lens pointing upwards at his face, he looked into the viewfinder lens. The viewfinder screen, pointing forward from the camera, conveyed a picture to the viewfinder lens which, in its inverted position, could be mistaken for the viewfinder screen. With the camera held accidentally in this position, Mrs Richards would have thought she was taking a photograph of the grave whereas the upturned lens proper would be capturing a chest-level view of her own face.

I returned to the Rhondda and gave Ivor Richards the explanation of the photograph. At first sceptical of what I had to tell him, he later expressed relief. I avoided reminding him that he had described his wife's nose as 'like the thumb of a boxing glove'.

Running a 'readers' requests' column for the *Daily Herald*, twenty-seven-year-old journalist Peter Small chuckled as he told me that one of the letters on his desk was from a man who wanted to go ghost-hunting. Could I take them with me on one of my nocturnal missions?

After a warming curry dinner in the West End, we arrived, just after 11 p.m., at rambling, sixteenth-century Hall Place in Bexley, Kent. Reputably haunted by a 'grey lady' said to be the earthbound spirit of a damsel who had committed suicide by throwing herself from the tower of the building after seeing her fiancé gored to death by a stag in the grounds, the old mansion was unlit, unheated and unfurnished. Having had it on my list of potential inquiries for some time, I had arranged facilities for our visit with the owners, the local council. I was required to sign an undertaking absolving them from all responsibility for anything that might happen to us in the building.

We were admitted by a caretaker who explained that, as he did not stay on duty all night, he would have to lock us in. His colleague would arrive at 6 a.m. to release us.

Having chosen a ground-floor 'base room', I explained and demonstrated the business of window- and door-sealing, intruder-proofing large chimneys and other routine investigatory measures. I emphasized the need, when introducing newcomers to the scene of a supposed haunting, to minimize the element of suggestion by providing no advance information as to the nature of the alleged phenomena. For this reason, I pointed out, I could give them no particulars as to what, if anything, might be expected to happen during our vigil. We settled down on three folding chairs we had brought with us, the *Herald* reader, Peter Granville, nervously clutching a large torch.

Small's article told the story:

> At exactly 2.25 am *it happens*. There is an echoing crash of a door banging closed.
>
> 'Probably the wind,' says Philip, leaning over backwards to be objective.
>
> 'Wind nothing,' says Peter. 'It's as still as a tomb outside.'
>
> 'Don't say tomb,' I barked. 'Anything but tomb – or corpse.'
>
> There is no wind. The trees are clamped white, frigid and unmoving in the grip of a brilliant moon.
>
> A chilling draught sneaks round our legs. But we have sealed the door with a blanket! I crouch back in my seat. Imagination, that's what it is. Only natural in a place like this.
>
> Philip flashes his torch at his thermometer on the wall. It has dropped four degrees in 10 minutes.
>
> We sit tight, Peter and I very close together. Philip has his ear squeezed to the corridor wall.
>
> Then – the thuds. I hear them, but say nothing until I feel Peter start.
>
> 'It's thuds,' says Peter, a trifle hoarsely. Being of a suspicious nature, I flash my torch from Peter to Philip – but neither is moving a muscle.
>
> Every 12 seconds – *thutch, thutch, thutch*. After two minutes – silence. A thick, heavy silence that seems to corrode into your brain. The thermometer is back to normal.
>
> Philip tells us the legend of Hall Place ... Her restless spirit is supposed to wander round the house with much rustling of skirts and *banging of doors*.
>
> Is that what we heard? Safe and sound and warm again, I like to think not. But I wouldn't relish spending a night alone in the place.

A week or two later I had to tell him that the sounds had been of very normal origin. Information had come my way that, to retrieve an item of personal property he had inadvertently left behind, the caretaker had returned to the house that night. Happily unperturbed – his usual disposition – Peter said it didn't matter at all. His reader's wish had been granted and some purpose served. We became firm friends, often meeting during his later engagement with the magazine *New Scientist*.

Sadly, the jocular words he had penned about 'tomb' and 'corpse' were later tragically recalled. Eight years afterwards he was himself a corpse, his tomb a diving-bell deep in the Pacific off Santa Catalina, California. A founder member of the British Sub Aqua Club, he had always been fascinated by the underwater world. And his lamentable death was soon followed by another. Broken-hearted by her loss which, helpless, she had witnessed on closed-circuit television in a boat, his twenty-three-year-old wife, Mary, killed herself in her London flat.

Asked by the news editor of the *News Chronicle* to investigate strange disturbances that were said to have driven a Loughborough, Leicestershire, family out of their home, I was taken to the scene by a *Chronicle* reporter of easily remembered by-line – Matt White. Matt was the epitome of the film-world newsman – snap-brimmed trilby, fawn trench-coat and portable typewriter case covered with hotel-labels from exotic places.

The house was a cramped and grubby terraced cottage in a gloomy back-street. Uninviting outside, it was still less encouraging within. Finding myself scratching two flea-bites only minutes after our arrival, I commented to Matt that we appeared to be in for a lively night of a kind other than we might have expected. Already hammering on his much-travelled typewriter, he nodded agreement.

Reflecting that I had never seen a stronger case for the invention of a 'ghost' as a means of gaining improved accommodation, I indicated to my companion that I felt our stay need not be too prolonged. But Matt was grimly determined to 'see it through'. The tenants having gone to stay with relatives, we were left to our own devices.

More as a means of passing time than for any serious purpose, I went through the motions of sealing doors and windows, marking the positions of small objects and so on. It was a long and intensely uncomfortable night. Twice there were noises that jerked Matt into eager alertness. On both occasions I was able to show him that they were caused by mice.

Then, in the early hours, there were much stronger sounds from the upper floor. With Matt on my heels, I made a speedy check. All my seals were intact, and everywhere the house seemed deserted. Acting on impulse, I heaved a heavy wardrobe away from a bedroom wall. It revealed a gaping hole that provided a view through to a bedroom of the semi-derelict dwelling next door. While shifting the wardrobe, I thought I detected sounds of swift movement from the other side of the wall. Peering through the hole with my torch, I saw signs of very human occupation. A tattered jacket hung from a nail above a bed of tumbled rags. A clutter of empty bottles was scattered over the floor. A cigarette end smouldered in an old saucer.

Professional to the core, Matt wrote a 'what was it?' story. It appeared only in the *Chronicle*'s northern editions.

16. Across a Psychic Sea

Although my travels in the USA have taken me across that continent, to such destinations as Los Angeles, San Francisco, California's capital Sacramento, the Sierra Nevada and Portland, Oregon, it seems that the north-eastern seaboard, with its still-surviving strong links with Europe, remains a focal point for psychic oddities in that vast land. It was at their home in Hydesville, New York State, that the Fox sisters, Margaretta and Katherine, produced the rappings that led to the foundation of modern Spiritualism.

Among other promptings that took me to New York was a wish to see the setting of strange experiences reported by a tense and tormented actress/poet named Janine Bryant Bartell.

Initial information reached me in an oddly roundabout way. Returning from a business conference in Germany, my wife, Joan, was engaged in conversation by a fellow-passenger seated next to her on the flight. An engineer involved in oil exploration in the Middle East, he was returning on leave to his home in Hull. Some of their talk concerned a paperback book he had been reading, entitled *Spindrift*. Not on sale in the UK and described in the cover blurb as 'the most terrifying book you will ever read' and 'the most unusual and frightening book of our time', it was Janine Bryant Bartell's story of encounters with alarming oddities over a period of sixteen years. Joan expressed her interest in it. Having finished with the work, the man gave it to her.

Written with a glitteringly descriptive vocabulary, it told an extraordinary tale in a style as taut as a piano wire. It began when, with her restaurant manager husband and a beloved but ailing Irish terrier, Penelope, the author moved into a top-floor flat in West Tenth Street, in New York's Montmartre, Greenwich Village. The tall house, one of a row of converted mansions, stands between one that was once the home of Samuel Langhorne Clemens – 'Mark Twain' – and another where the frail young Emma Lazarus, writer of the noble sentiments enshrined at the base of the Statue of Liberty ('Give me your tired, your poor, your huddled masses yearning to breathe free ... ') suffered a lingering death from cancer.

On the first night of their occupancy, lying on her bed facing a white wall in a moonlit room, Janine was terrified by 'a monstrous shadow that loomed up from behind me'. Her screams brought her husband to her side. (A World War II veteran of Guadalcanal, Leyte and the Philippines, he suffered from recurrent bouts of dengue fever; for that reason the couple slept in separate rooms.) A down-to-earth person, he tried, unsuccessfully, to persuade her that the shadow had been caused by a bird flying through the moonlight.

Her discovery, in a cupboard, of a box of broken Sèvres, Limoges, Chelsea and Wedgwood crockery that had been abandoned by the previous occupier, a dealer in antiques, added to her forebodings – 'These things were broken because they had been thrown at something – or someone ... ' Next, she began hearing unaccountable footsteps in the flat. A heavy smoker, she turned to Seconal and Valium for relief from her growing anxieties.

There were also poltergeist-like incidents. When she was entertaining a friend to dinner one evening, both heard an enormous crash like breaking crockery. But nothing was found broken. Later the same evening, when Janine was out of the room, her visitor heard 'a rustling' and 'sensed a presence' behind her.

Janine's fears were further heightened when a cleaning woman told her she had seen a mysterious 'woman in white' in the apartment. Then, while washing up after a meal with her husband, she found a dried grape resting in the centre of a plate she had minutes earlier seen to be empty. Again trying to soothe her distress, he told her a mouse could have dropped it.

Penelope's final sickness brought Janine's spirits lower still. Having heard of Sylvia Barbanell's book *When Your Animal Dies*, she had ordered a copy from a nearby bookshop. The man who delivered it told her, in frightened tones, that he had been followed up the stairs by an invisible something. 'Is this house haunted?' he asked as he hurried away.

A second cleaning woman said she had seen a grey cat dash into the bathroom. The Bartells had no cat. In the street, Janine saw 'a ball of light' that was evidently invisible to others – a woman passer-by walked through it. The cleaning woman, who claimed to have Red Indian blood, commented on a persistent odour in the flat as being 'like sumpin' daid'. With the dog that had replaced Penelope, Janine fled into pouring rain. On another occasion, the dog uttered 'a moan of terror' and, watched by both the Bartells, appeared to follow the movement of someone or something invisible to them. During their last night in the flat (they lived there for almost seven years), Janine saw the shape of a man in black – 'like the figure on the label of Sandeman's sherry' – move towards her, drift over her head and vanish through a window.

After three years at other addresses they moved back to West Tenth Street – into the top-floor apartment of the Mark Twain house. An unnerving series of deaths followed. A woman living on the ground floor committed suicide. An elderly man on the third floor died. His wife, going blind, killed herself. A tenant living on the second floor was attacked, robbed and fatally injured in the vestibule. Shortly afterwards, his wife was found dead. Another tenant was found to have terminal cancer. Janine's husband was taken dangerously ill with peritonitis and pneumonia. When he recovered, they moved to Westchester Village. Soon afterwards, the owner of the Mark Twain house died, and this was followed by her husband's death, in the basement of the building.

The most poignant event was, however, still to come. A month after delivering the manuscript of her book to the publisher, Janine died, alone, in her home in New Rochelle. The coroner's report gave the cause of death as a heart attack. The troubled spirit was quietened at last.

Beguiled by the depth of feeling behind her flowing, agonized words, I set about making inquiries aimed at discovering whether anyone else had encountered the intensity of experience she had suffered in her West Tenth Street homes.

Though Greenwich Village is not what it once was, the neighbourhood retains the subtle ambience of an artistic quarter in one of the world's most dynamic cities. I walked the pavements of the area trying to imagine the place as it was in the time of Clemens and Lazarus and endeavouring to see its modernization as it would have appeared to Janine. I climbed, with some effort, the flights of steep stairs that led to her former eyries. I spoke with people living in the houses that she had found so filled with sinister menace. I met no one who claimed experiences or feelings like hers. All were friendly, matter-of-fact folk preoccupied with the business of living.

Soon, the lady and her story were enigmas no more. The fine

tuning that had produced her super-sensitivity and a personality that had her retching after only the mildest tiff with her ever-patient husband had left its own clues. This had not been a lady who lived in haunted houses. This had been a haunted lady. As she said in *Spindrift*: ' ... a vast psychic sea must be crossed before we can come home to ourselves.' Janine Bartell deserves to have reached her haven.

17. Amityville: Horror or Outrage?

Early in 1976 news reports of a haunting with elements of exceptional terror swept across the Atlantic. Later the story appeared in a book – *The Amityville Horror* – that became an international best-seller. Serialized versions were published in newspapers and magazines. A film reproducing – with some profound discrepancies – the alleged events drew packed audiences into the cinemas of many nations. The young married couple who claimed to have suffered the violent attentions of paranormal forces told their story in radio and television appearances in Britain and elsewhere. Although the happenings they described covered a period of only twenty-eight days, the publicity that followed must have displaced Borley, with all its years of oddities, as the most widely known case of its kind on earth.

The focal point of the drama was a six-bedroomed Dutch colonial style house built in 1928 in an affluent avenue in the Long Island, New York, village of Amityville, some thirty miles east of Brooklyn. Backing onto the Amityville river, the property stands on a plot measuring 237 by 50 feet and includes a heated swimming pool, two-car garage and 45 by 22 foot boathouse.

In 1974 the place was owned by forty-three-year-old car-dealer Ronald DeFeo, who occupied it with his forty-two-year-old wife Louise, his twenty-two-year-old son Ronald, eighteen- and thirteen-year-old daughters Dawn and Allison, and twelve- and seven-year-old sons Mark and John. At 3.15 a.m. on 14 November Ronald junior, using a high-powered rifle, shot his mother, father, sisters and brothers to death in their beds. At his trial, he said he had 'heard voices' in the house, but later admitted that this was only a story he had told to foster the idea that he was mentally ill when committing the murders. Some people believed his motives to have been a $200,000 life insurance policy and a cache of money said to have been hidden in his parents' bedroom. At the time of the crime he had a previous conviction for theft and was on probation for a drug offence. He and his father were known to have had violent quarrels but he was thought to be fond of his mother and brothers and sisters. Despite a defence plea of insanity, he was sentenced to six consecutive terms of life imprisonment – a total of 150 years.

In December 1975 the house was sold for $80,000 – then equivalent to some £40,000 – to twenty-eight-year-old George Lutz, a former corporal in the US marine corps and in civilian life owner of a land-surveying agency. With his thirty-year-old wife Kathleen and her three children by a previous marriage (two boys, aged seven and nine, and a girl aged five), he moved in on 18 December, bringing belongings from their previous home about fourteen miles away. He also purchased some of the DeFeo family's bedroom and dining-room furniture.

The Lutzes knew about the murders and believed that the low price asked for the house was attributable to the tragedy. Originally looking for a cheaper property, Lutz had to raise a substantial mortgage to make the purchase. He was said to be experiencing some financial anxieties with his business affairs and, a Methodist by upbringing, was reported as having, for two years, been practising transcendental meditation. His wife, a Roman Catholic, was said to have been accompanying him in that pursuit for a year.

They decided that, of the two top-floor rooms, one would serve as a bedroom for the boys and the other as the children's playroom. On the first floor, a room diagonally opposite their master bedroom would be occupied by the girl, while the rooms in the other corners of that floor would be used for dressing and sewing.

Of the book recording the experiences that were reported to have followed, a reviewer wrote in a British Sunday newspaper: 'One of the most terrifying true cases ever of haunting and possession by demons ... breathless ... heartstopping ... chilling ... a huge bestseller.' Among the American reviewers, a writer for the *Kansas City Star* promised: 'This book will scare the hell out of you,' while the *Los Angeles Times* reacted with: 'A fascinating, frightening book ... the scariest true story I have read in years.'

The massive publicity began on 5 February 1976, less than three weeks after the Lutzes had left the house. A New York television station having announced that it would be showing a series on psychics, one of its reporters described his investigation of the Amityville affair. Tragedy had, it was said, struck earlier residents in the dwelling, though no details of those events were given. The programme presenter added that, with a view to obtaining a retrial for his client, the lawyer representing DeFeo was hoping to prove that some inexplicable force influenced the behaviour of people occupying the property.

Two weeks later, the Lutzes held a Press conference in the lawyer's office. Lutz said that, although he would not return to the house, he was not proposing to dispose of it at once; he was awaiting the outcome of tests by parapsychologists. Soon afterwards he and his family departed to a secret location in California, where they became incommunicado. It was reported that they abandoned all their belongings in the house, with the exception of clothing, and that Lutz signed his interest in the property over to the mortgagor bank.

I was struck by the fact that none of the statements describing the case made any significant mention of the possibility of some rational explanation. Finding this strange, I decided to make inquiries. Kindly accommodated by my friends Bernard and Jeanette Rosen in their home at Yonkers, a northern suburb of New York City, I was driven to Amityville along the monotonous route that skirts the flat southern shore of Long Island. I found the house, by then resold, among others of similar standard in a pleasing neighbourhood of fresh white paint, neatly trimmed shrubs and carefully tended lawns.

Although I was received politely, it was apparent that I was unwelcome. It soon became clear that life for the new owners was made nightmarish by the persistent attentions of numerous morbid sightseers – the usual result of publicity in such matters. (I have more to say of this later.) Trying to minimize my intrusion, I kept my questions to essentials. As is invariably the case, the new occupiers had experienced nothing untoward in the house, which they considered to be an entirely normal habitation.

When dissected, the events said to have occurred during the Lutzes' twenty-eight-day residence can be seen to amount to some eighty-five incidents. Of these, thirty were recorded as the uncorroborated 'feelings' or other experiences of individuals, the most difficult form of evidence to verify or dismiss. There were also said to have been forty-nine paranormal physical occurrences witnessed by more than one person at the same time. Added to these were four statements attributed to the children and two instances of what was considered to be paranormally induced irrational behaviour by Lutz.

To analyse this material it is necessary to examine it item by item.

The following is a chronological list, to which I have appended notes suggesting potential explanations of normal causes.

18 Dec.

1 *A Roman Catholic priest had a nervous reaction when invited to bless the house.*

2 *In the house the priest heard a disembodied voice tell him to leave.*

3 *The priest felt exhausted and unwell.* He had learned that the house was the former DeFeo home only just before going there. The shock may have caused him to expect unusual events. He was also developing influenza. No corroborative evidence.

4 *After leaving, the priest found his car being propelled to the edge of the road, then the bonnet and door flew open and the car stalled.* The car was old and worn.

5 *The windscreen wipers worked without being switched on in a car used by another cleric to rescue the priest from his broken-down vehicle.* Could have been an electrical or mechanical fault.

19-21 Dec.

6 *Lutz heard raps.* The house is constructed largely of wood, an organic material subject to expansion and shrinkage, especially during sharp variations of temperature and humidity.

7 *Lutz saw something move near the boathouse. Dog barked when he shouted.*

8 *Lutz heard more knocks.* The boathouse door was blowing in the wind.

9 *Lutz shouted at the children; complained of feeling cold; turned the central heating temperature up to 75° F.* He had business and financial worries added to the upheaval of moving.

22 Dec.

10 *Something unseen embraced Kathleen Lutz and patted her hand.* She must by this time have been aware that her husband was suffering stress. The power of suggestion/-expectation is strong. No corroborative evidence.

11 *A black substance was found in the second-floor toilet pan.*

12 *A similar substance was found in the first-floor toilet.* Foulness sometimes develops in the plumbing systems of

properties left unoccupied for lengthy periods. The house had been empty for a year. The first-floor toilet is immediately below that on the second floor and may have been similarly contaminated by a gravitational effect. Also children may have put something into the toilets.

13 *A mass of flies was found on the sewing-room window.* Lutz had increased the central heating temperature to 80° F. The room contained two radiators. The sudden increase in temperature in a long-empty house could have brought about incubation of the flies.

14 *The front door was found hanging on one hinge.* Gale force winds were blowing.

15 *The children were seen sleeping on their stomachs – the position in which the DeFeo murder victims were said to have been found.* Coincidence.

16 *The boys fought.* Picking up anxieties from mother and stepfather? Childish squabbles are natural.

17 *There was a sour smell in a bedroom cupboard.* A dead rodent behind the panelling? (Premises on a river bank.) Decomposition accelerated by central heating temperature?

18 *A crucifix was inverted in a cupboard.* High winds were shaking the house.

24 Dec.

19 *Telephoning the Lutzes, the priest heard much crackling and interference on the line.* The telephone wires are carried on poles. Gale-force winds were blowing.

20 *The Lutzes and some visitors felt cold and draughts.* It was winter, in a rambling, neglected house.

21 *Lutz found the sewing-room window open, more flies there.* The window was the up-and-down sliding 'sash' type. A loose catch, vibration and sudden wind pressure might cause upper section to fall open. Also see 13 above.

22 *The Lutzes and visitors heard a crack from boathouse door.* Wind and a faulty lock? A workman recalled that DeFeo had had trouble with the lock.

25 Dec.

23 *Disturbed, Lutz went to the boathouse soon after 3 a.m. There was a full moon. Looking up at his stepdaughter's window, he saw her face and that of a huge pig looking out.*

Rushing to her bedroom, he found her asleep in bed, but her little rocking chair was moving. By this time Lutz must have been in a highly tense state. Even in normal conditions it is easy to be misled by the reflections of moonlight on a window. The movement of the tiny rocking chair could have been caused by the draught of his hasty entry into the bedroom or the vibration of his hurried footsteps on the floor. No corroborative evidence.

24 *The little girl told her elder brother she had a friend in the house – a pig.*

25 *Girl told her mother she was talking to the pig.* Lutz must have told his wife about his horrendous sighting of the pig. Did his stepdaughter overhear such mention, as children often eavesdrop on adult conversations? Or was it simply a small child's fantasy?

26 *The dog was sleepy.* Animals' health varies, as does humans'.

26 Dec.

27 *Lutz had a stomach upset.* A physical symptom of stress?

28 *Kathleen sensed a presence behind her, smelt perfume, then felt that she was touched by an unseen female.* Heightened imagination and nervousness? No corroborative evidence.

29 *A visitor lost an envelope containing money from the pocket of a coat left on a chair.* Was this really lost in the house or, unknowingly, mislaid elsewhere? The details of such losses can easily become confused or mistaken.

27 Dec.

30 *A visitor (a former nun) refused to enter the sewing-room or playroom, and left early.* The lady was clearly acting in accordance with her own instincts or superstitions. No proof of paranormality.

31 *A small boy from a neighbouring family wouldn't play upstairs with the Lutz children.* Child may have been shy with strangers he had just met or felt uncomfortable in the atmosphere of the house.

32 *The Lutzes found a secret room under stairs.* Since every stairway must have a space beneath it, this four by five foot enclosure could hardly be described as a secret room.

33 *Seeing a face appear on plywood in a cupboard next to the 'secret' room, Lutz identified it as Ronald DeFeo, the*

murderer. With a heightened imagination it is easy to 'see' faces in fires, wallpaper patterns or the grain of wood. Ronald DeFeo is still alive, serving his prison sentence at Dannemora, in the north of New York State.

28 Dec.

34 *An employee in a local bar, where DeFeo first told of committing the murders, commented on Lutz's resemblance to the killer*. Clearly pure coincidence.

35 *Kathleen thought she saw a large ceramic lion ornament move towards her*. Further evidence of suggestion/-expectation/stress? No corroborative evidence.

36 *There were more difficulties with the Lutz and priest's telephones*. See comment under 19 above.

37 *Lutz fell against logs in fireplace and received teeth-like marks on his ankle*. Striking flesh against rough wood might produce what appear to be teeth-marks.

29 Dec.

38 *Shock-absorber fell off Lutz's van*. Comment unnecessary.

39 *Kathleen thought she heard a window being opened and closed in sewing-room but dared not investigate*. Children at play or imagined noises?

40 *Wheel loose on Lutz's van and jack handle missing*. Comment unnecessary.

41 *The priest, suffering from influenza, developed red marks on the palms of his hands*. He was running a high temperature and feeling increasingly anxious about his physical and mental condition.

30 Dec.

42 *Local historical society said to have told Lutz that Indians had used nearby land as a 'death enclosure' for the sick, mad and terminally ill, also that a Satanist forced out of Salem, Massachusetts, during the infamous witch-hunt there had lived within five hundred feet of the house while continuing his alleged devil-worship*. Did these statements (which were later denied) help to explain the oddities or merely add to the Lutzes' growing fears and conviction that almost everything they saw or heard was sinister?

1 Jan.

43 *Kathleen saw a devil in flames in the fireplace.* See comment under 33 above.

44 *Windows found open in the Lutzes' bedroom and the sewing- and dressing-rooms.* All the windows concerned were of the sliding sash type. Violent gusts of wind were blowing. See comment under 21 above.

45 *After he had poked the embers of the living-room fire and turned off the lights, Lutz and his wife saw what appeared to be red eyes looking in through the window. They disappeared when the lights were switched on again. Outside, they found hoofprints in the snow like those of a huge pig.* Several potential explanations are available. First, small glowing embers must have remained in the fire. These could have caused reflections appearing as red eyes in the window, which would have disappeared when the lights were switched on again. Second, it is improbable that the eyes – if eyes they were – could have been those of a pig. The coloured luminescence seen in the eyes of certain animals at night is caused by a lustrous opaque structure between the vascular and capillary layers in the posterior part of the eye, called the *tapetum lucidum.* Its function is to aid the vision of nocturnally active creatures. According to H.H. Dukes, professor of veterinary physiology at New York State Veterinary College, Cornell University, in his *Physiology of Domestic Animals*, 'It occurs in all domestic animals *except the pig*' (my italics). This fact was confirmed for me by Dr Roger Curtiss of the British Animal Health Trust. Third, as to the prints in the snow, certain types of animal tracks may easily be mistaken for those of other species. My inquiries in Amityville unearthed the fact that a while earlier a wild deer, of which there are numbers elsewhere on the island, had been seen in the village. Deer have hooves which leave imprints similar to those of pigs. Deer also possess the *tapetum lucidum.* Fourth, the footprints in snow of swans, geese and certain other web-footed birds can resemble the prints of cloven hooves. Swans, Canadian geese and other large aquatic birds are plentiful on the Amityville River and have a habit of coming ashore for protection during the winter shooting season.

2 Jan.

46 *The prints were still visible in the frozen snow, ending at the entrance to the garage, the door of which was almost torn from its frame. The prints and damaged door were said to have been inspected by Detective Sergeant Pat Cammaroto of Amityville Police Department, who was also reported to have been shown the secret room and was described as experiencing a creepy feeling and strong vibrations in the house.* Detective Sergeant Cammaroto gave me a signed statement making it clear that he never visited the house during the Lutzes' brief residence and adding that the report of his inspection of the prints, damaged door and secret room and reactions inside the building was, therefore, totally untrue. As to the damage to the door, high winds were still blowing.

47 *Kathleen felt herself grasped around her waist then by her wrists.* See comments under 10 and 28 above. No corroborative evidence.

48 *The priest was assailed by the stench of excrement which he believed accompanied the presence of the devil.*

49 *Lutz was afflicted by a similar smell.* Sewage disposal in the area was by cesspools; sewers have only recently been installed in Amityville. Wind-blown winter tides, coupled with a varying water table, may have caused 'throwbacks' of human waste and odour. There is also a well in the basement of the house, which may have been fouled.

3 Jan.

50 *A normally placid pastor squabbled with the priest.* Human temperaments vary and are sometimes aggravated by bad weather.

51 *The ceramic lion, which had been taken upstairs, was found in the living-room.* Moved by children?

4/5 Jan.

52 *Lutz heard martial music coming from downstairs rooms in the middle of the night. When he went down, the noises stopped. Back upstairs, he found his wife, still sleeping, levitated above their bed.* A stress-induced nightmare? No corroborative evidence.

5 Jan.

53 *While outside the house, Lutz heard a band start playing within, accompanied by the stamping of feet. Indoors he found furniture had been moved. The noises stopped when he entered.* Another stress experience? No corroborative evidence.

54 *The friend who had helped the priest after his car breakdown reported receiving an anonymous telephone call threatening the priest with death if he returned to the house.* News about the oddities must have been spreading in the area. A crank in action?

6 Jan.

55 *The dog refused to stay with the little girl in her room.* Dogs normally kept outdoors are often unhappy in houses.

56 *Lutz again saw his wife levitated above their bed.*

57 *Her face appeared like that of an old crone. When Kathleen looked in a mirror, there were long black creases down her cheeks. In the morning her appearance had returned to normal.* Stress, exhaustion and nightmares?

7 Jan.

58 *Lutz found a bannister broken on the second-floor landing.* Boisterous children?

8/9 Jan.

59 *A female visitor, sleeping with her husband in the little girl's room, woke screaming that she had seen a phantom boy sitting on the foot of the bed.* Nightmare induced by the atmosphere in the house? Her husband, who saw nothing unusual, said it was a dream.

60 *The Lutzes heard a humming sound while they were 'blessing' the house. (The priest had refused to return.)*

61 *Lutz heard a disembodied voice say 'Will you stop.'* Heightened expectations during their 'blessing' effort?

9 Jan.

62 *Green gelatinous spots were found on walls, trickling down to the floor.* Some mischief by children, who were too frightened to admit the prank? Why wasn't some of the substance kept for examination?

63 *Lutz reacted angrily when his wife suggested leaving the house.* Anxiety and frustration at his lack of control over events?

64 *Flames sprang from the fireplace at Lutz, who then felt an unaccountable nudge in his back.* Flames: an errant gust of wind in chimney? Touch in back: Nervous reaction after fright by flames?

65 *Windows found open in children's bedrooms.* See comment under 44 above. Lutz had earlier thrown all windows open and told the invading presence to depart.

10 Jan.

66 *Kathleen found ugly red streaks across her body.*

67 *While looking at the marks, she thought someone unseen was watching her.*

68 *The disfigurements disappeared the same day.* Skin eruptions are sometimes caused by nervous disturbance.

69 *Having opened her bedroom windows to air the room, Kathleen sent her nine-year-old son to shut them. His hand was caught under a window.* Sash windows can be heavy and stiff to push up and down. It would be easy for a child to trap a hand in such windows.

70 *Lutz was unable to call a doctor to attend to the boy's hand because the wind had blown down a telephone pole.* See 19 and 36 above.

71 *Winds threw the front door against the building. Lutz had difficulty in closing it.*

11 Jan.

72 *Windows and doors were found open; ten window panes were broken.* See comments under 14, 19, 21, 36, 44, 46 and 64 above. Much gale damage was done to trees in the area – many branches fell into surrounding roads. Lutz then nailed some windows closed and nailed closed the doors to the sewing-room and children's playroom.

73 *The dog didn't like the cellar when Lutz was touring the house with him after being told that animals are sensitive to paranormalities.* A dog not normally permitted in a house may fear punishment when in the building. It may also have disliked the odours in the cellar.

74 *Lutz, asleep, shouted that he was coming apart.* More evidence of stress and nervousness?

12 Jan.

75 *His little stepdaughter told Lutz that her friend the pig wanted to speak to him in her room.*

76 *In the room she said that he had had to go outside for a minute, then pointed to two red eyes looking in at the window. Terrified, Kathleen threw a play chair at the window, smashing it. There was a cry of pain and loud squealing and the eyes vanished. Nothing was visible outside, but the squeals appeared to be retreating towards the boathouse.* See comment under 45 above. The supposed eyes may have been reflections in the glass. The squealing may have been sounds made by a bird disturbed by the noise of the window being broken.

77 *Lutz again heard a band playing in the living-room, but Kathleen and the children, in the same bedroom with him, were not awakened.* See comment under 52 and 53 above. No corroborative evidence.

12/13 Jan.

78 *Lutz dreamt that a shadowy figure was attacking the younger boy in the boys' bedroom.* The child was then in same bedroom as his stepfather. Evidently a nightmare.

13 Jan

79 *Lutz saw a green substance emerging from a hole in the playroom door, where he had removed the lock. Taking off the boards he had used to nail up the door, he examined the room but found nothing unusual.* Again a children's prank? Because it would be easily within their reach, children would be likely to put substance into a lock hole. There is also something of a contradiction here – it was reported that, the previous day, a glazier had been in the 'nailed-up' room repairing damaged windows.

80 *Kathleen got out of bed while still asleep and the dog, chained in the bedroom doorway, was sick.* Comment unnecessary.

81 *Lutz believed he heard furniture moving in the boys' bedroom above and in his own room but was unable to move himself. Next came voices and the band again from downstairs. Although his bedroom door was swinging wildly, the dog slept near it and no one else awoke. The episode ended with what felt like animal hooves treading on him in*

bed. Further subjective experiences arising from stress? No corroborative evidence.

14 Jan.

82 *Boys told Lutz there was a demon in their room.*

83 *Investigating, he saw a massive figure in white.*

84 *Abandoning the house with Kathleen and the children, he found the front door open again and hanging on one hinge.* There had been another violent storm, with heavy sleet and rain. By this time, all the occupants of the house must have been subject to expectations of horrific proportions. Was the figure Lutz saw an effect of the weather, reflected into the house?

15/16 Jan.

85 *Staying at another house nearby, the Lutzes had a sensation of levitation off their bed and then saw a line of greenish black slime ascending stairs towards them.* What became of the substance? Who cleared it up? Why wasn't some kept for examination?

The purpose of a breakdown of this kind is to facilitate judgement as to which of the happenings claimed as paranormal might reasonably be regarded as being beyond any rational explanation. No alleged haunting can sensibly be judged on the basis of the total impression left by a collection of unexamined events. Each incident must be looked at separately so that the value of its contribution can be assessed. It is only by these means that a realistic overall conclusion becomes possible.

In my view, the experiences claimed by the Lutzes do not emerge well from such detailed scrutiny. None of the occurrences they reported is totally outside the possibility of normal cause. This is not to say that anyone was guilty of deliberate fabrication. The style in which the Lutzes' story was presented in its various forms and versions conveyed a genuine belief that they had received the unwelcome attentions of some menacing intelligence beyond human understanding. But some people who were physically close to the scene gave very different views. Amityville's village clerk, Gordon Moore, told me that he considered the whole thing 'hogwash', conceived and carried out for two purposes – to attempt to gain a sympathetic re-trial for DeFeo and to make money.

Although no re-trial was achieved, much money was certainly made. It was conservatively estimated that the Lutzes received at least $100,000 from the book – which sold five million copies – and a similar sum from the film. And lawyers were soon busy with quarrels. The next owners of the house brought an action against the Lutzes, alleging that their lives had been made intolerable by the visitations of sightseers attracted by the publicity. It is not difficult to imagine their sufferings. Moore told me that the appearance of the book and film cost the village several thousands of dollars in providing police protection of the property but, despite the officers' vigilance, determined curiosity-seekers succeeded in ripping souvenirs from the building.

After the new residents' claim had been settled out of court – for an undisclosed sum – the house was again sold, to a man who, it was said, had in mind its value as a tourist attraction. It did not, however, seem likely that the Amityville authorities would be willing to approve any scheme for such exploitation.

In what was, perhaps, the most bizarre move of all, the Lutzes themselves took legal action against the *New York Daily News*, claiming $4 million damages for 'invasion of privacy' after the paper had published an article describing their alleged experiences. The writers had, said the Lutzes, used their name for profit and caused them emotional distress. The suit was dismissed by a federal judge who ruled that the story was one of legitimate public interest in which the laws relating to invasion of privacy did not apply. He added that he found no negligence by the reporters in gathering their facts and rejected the 'profit' accusation because newspapers were entitled to use names and pictures in publishing truthful news stories.

In another lawsuit brought against the Lutzes, DeFeo's lawyer accused them of breach of contract in respect of failure to fulfil a promise to work with him in producing a novel called *Devil on my back*.

Amity had obviously deserted Amityville!

A journalist friend in New York told me that the Lutzes had taken up residence in a pleasant city in southern California. There were, he mentioned, reports that the Amityville evil had followed them! Later, two more books were published describing further paranormal sufferings the Lutzes were said to have experienced in their subsequent homes.

Few claims of haunting can have produced such a rich financial harvest – or given rise to such bitter formal disputes. But what of the truth of the matter? Some might say that, even if the entire affair was imagined or concocted, no real harm was done, since those who read the articles, bought the book, watched television, listened to the radio or paid to see the film must have received the spine-chilling thrills they were seeking. For the serious student the issue cannot be summed up so simply. The accounts were presented as records of fact. If they were fiction, they create the danger that natural human reactions will place more bricks in the barriers that have to be faced by those tormented by genuine poltergeist infestation. From this point of view, if they were erroneous, the Amityville chronicles will have been more of an outrage than a horror.

18. Epilogue

For in and out, above, below
'Tis nothing but a magic shadow-show
Played in a box whose candle is the sun
Round which we phantom figures come and go.

Omar Khayyam

What then, the reader will wish to know, are the conclusions I have drawn from my years of probing? Am I fully persuaded that there are such things as ghosts and poltergeists? If I am, do I believe that they demonstrate human survival of physical death?

Big questions that must be approached with a proper sense of perspective. First let me confess that I have received no divine disclosure. Like the reader, I am only an insignificant biped who has been permitted to crawl awhile on a speck of inconsequential dust spinning obscurely in a 100,000 million star galaxy. We are but mites of transient matter in creation's scheme. But we are part of the orchestra of being. Our bodies provide the worlds of the living creatures that exist upon us.

Functional value cannot be measured by physical dimension. Biological life is perpetuated by microscopical protoplasms which nevertheless contrive to embody the hereditary patterns of their originators. You and I were once but specks invisible to the naked eye. The mightiest oak was once but an acorn, the largest whale once just a few exiguous cells.

Behaviour incorporates other marvels. Guided by knowledge that confounds our fathoming, tiny fish cross vast oceans to predetermined destinations. Little birds move half across the world at the call of a seasonal time-clock. While man's ingenuity has taken him on some querulous steps beyond the gravitational influence of earth, he has yet to succeed in creating artificially one drop of blood or a single blade of grass.

Time is a grand illusion. What is a single lifespan of exploration – or a thousand such lifespans – related to the mysteries that have baffled us since we first acquired the ability to reason? And by what right may we suppose that the strains from which we sprang were the first human cultures on this planet? Our knowledge of the past is fractional compared with the geologically measured age of the world. The clues of palaeontology help but little. Who would dare to guarantee that, between cataclysms, the globe has not nurtured many civilizations?

These things are part of the backcloth that needs to be kept in mind when considering the so-called paranormal. Its study, nowadays categorized as parapsychology, is only slowly gaining the 'respectability' of scientific recognition. But scientific ventures in the field often produce unsatisfactory results. The reasons are not hard to find. The basic requirements of formalistic science are that phenomena must conform to standard precepts and be reproducible on demand. Occult ordinances do not function so. They cannot be forced into preconceived patterns or compelled to perform in accordance with investigatory wills. Not least among the difficulties is the fact that the attitudes commonly found among orthodox scientists have been shown to be inhibitive of psychic phenomena.

'Clever' words have been introduced to explain away events that cannot be slotted into standard pigeon-holes: hallucination, hysteria, animal magnetism, delusion, optical or auditory malfunctions, glandular disturbances, mental disorders. When high-flown terminology is patently inapplicable, more mundane diagnoses are available: malobservation, fraudulence, practical jokes, sleight-of-hand, superstition.

These comments should not be misinterpreted. I am no advocate of credulity. Without doubt, each of the foregoing verdicts is sometimes correct. But scrutiny should be carried out with patience, coupled with the admission that human intelligence is limited and fallible. Above all, inquiries should proceed unfettered by dogma. Open minds find more pathways than prejudiced pre-notions. The scoffers and the ill-informed are invariably the same people.

Let me preface my answers to the primary questions with a truism used by thinking Spiritualists: personal convictions are rarely born from the testimonies of others. The conclusions that follow are not, therefore, oracular; I am still learning. My opinions seem to me to represent the most valid reasoning currently available to account for the things I have examined. I am always willing to hearken to judgements based on superior logic.

So am I persuaded that there are such things as ghosts and poltergeists? The years that have passed since I answered Harding have produced nothing to cause me to alter the reply I gave him. But, as I would have done then had there been time, I must add a word or two of explanation.

In my view, the evidence for the appearance of phantoms, sometimes recognized as representations of people living or dead and sometimes unidentifiable, is overwhelming. How and why they occur no one knows. There are, however, indications that the ethereal images of people who were, in life, strongly attached to specific persons, buildings or localities, continue, for varying periods, to manifest in those environs.

Sometimes the spirit hypothesis (i.e., survival of physical death) would seem to be among the admissible explanations. It is weakened by the instances in which the phantoms of persons still living (though usually either sleeping or subject to some crisis) are seen. A concept that might cater for both categories is the notion of an 'etheric' counterpart of the physical body which, under certain circumstances, is able to wander from the material original, living or dead.

Some link with sleep seems likely. Since, during slumber, the mind is unaware of the body though still supported by it, it is reasonable to regard sleep as a condition partway towards death. Some religious philosophies speak of each day's awakening as a new life. There have been many claims of 'astral travelling' whilst under general anaesthesia, some of them seemingly corroborated by remarkable recapitulations of conversations overheard by deeply insensible patients in operating theatres.

'Thought-forms' occurring in the minds of percipients may account for some 'sightings' of phantoms, despite the fact that the witnesses declare they were not then thinking of the person whose figure was seen.

As to poltergeists, no serious student can long remain in doubt that these disturbing invasions occur. But what, and why, are they? Are they really 'noisy spirits' or merely the manifestation of some terrestrial energy that has so far eluded our understanding?

My answer, which is not meant to be evasive, is that they can equally validly be attributed to either or both. This foot-in-two-camps stance arises from the wide variations observable in the characteristics of the happenings. In some cases there is no sign of anything other than a random outbreak of unregulated turmoil. In others there are clear demonstrations of the operation of a sentient awareness.

There are no rules by which infestations can be measured or classified, any more than there is a specification of the conditions that must apply before phenomena can occur. Old and new premises of many kinds are similarly affected. Sometimes children passing through puberty are present, sometimes not. The one common trait which appears to apply in virtually all cases is that outbreaks begin in a minor key, build up to a crescendo and then fade out. There is no record of any serious physical injury being caused directly to man, woman or infant, despite a catalogue of severe damage to property. Other animals are sometimes tragically stricken. Whatever he, she or it may be, there can be no doubt that the poltergeist operates among us.

My response to the question of survival of physical death has to be more complicated. As the reader is aware, this is a work of fact not philosophy. But the psychical investigator who confines himself strictly to analysis of events, granting no time to the consideration of theoretical possibilities, puts himself in the position of an astronomer who, denying Copernicus, Kepler, Galileo and Newton, declares that, despite its known limitations, his telescope sees all.

Obviously, pitting the mind against the scabrous enigma of death calls for standards of judgement. But there is no unquestionable specification of what those standards must be. Individuals have to decide their own. Thus, material that satisfies John will not necessarily persuade Joe. As some men are born hopeful, others are created doubtful. So it is that, to many psychical researchers, the Spiritualist appears as the ingenuous victim of his own wishful thinking, while to most Spiritualists the psychical researcher looms as bigoted and destructive.

As I have said, it is well established that certain attitudes are inhibitors of psychic phenomena. I have seen many examples of previously active seance-room phenomena reduced to impotent quiescence by the presence of some sneering sceptic. It is an aspect that raises further significant questions. For example, to what extent should one be 'sympathetic' in conducting one's inquiries? How far should one be prepared to extend a helping hand for the purpose of achieving results? At what point do such aids step over the borderline of objectivity and invite deception or delusion?

Broadening these conjectures, the thinker encounters more groundwork. Is it reasonable to suppose that the promise of survival, the basis of most religions, is no more than a device aimed at restraining behaviour on earth? Is it acceptable to conclude that the only purpose of the lives of the hordes who have preceded us was to serve as links in the biological chain? Is extinction the only promise of birth?

If the unpalatableness of the questions leads to the theory 'there must be more to it than that', other complexities ensue. What of the flora and fauna with which we – often parasitically – share our planet? At what point, if any, on the scale of living things from mammoth to microbe does body exist without soul? The *post mortem* fate of humanity cannot be the single concern.

Nor can acceptance of the idea of an after-life be the end of the puzzle. Having vacated its exhausted physical shell, what is the future for the psyche? Does it rest for ever in idyllic delicacy? Does it, like a shout or a radio wave, persist only for a time before absorption into a limitless vacuum? Does it go on to inhabit another physique, on earth or elsewhere? Does it have a choice, or suffer direction, between these courses? Are the reincarnationists right in their notions of young and old souls, the latter accounting for genius in infancy and the recognition of places previously unvisited in current lifetimes? And who is to gainsay the possibility that some people survive death while others do not?

It is not easy to resist the expectation that any form of communication from the other side of the Great Adventure should bring with it revelations of profundity. Rare though they are, some such cases are said to have occurred. One of the most notable to come to my attention is reported to have happened in an Italian village. A married woman in her early forties expired, plunging her large family into the extreme demonstrations of grief that are usual in that part of the world. Such was the distress of some of her closest relatives that, keeping the business secret from the priest, they arranged a seance in the hope of contacting the dead woman. The effort proved frighteningly successful. A communicator claiming to be the deceased informed them that she had been buried alive, a deep coma having been mistaken for death. She had, she told her horrified listeners, recovered consciousness only to find herself trapped in the hopeless darkness of her coffin. There, she had suffered a dreadful death from the combined effects of shock and suffocation. Appalled, those who had attended the seance debated frantically among themselves as to what they should do. At last they told the priest what had happened. Deciding that it was the only way to silence their growing hysteria, he persuaded the authorities to permit exhumation.

When the coffin was opened, a terrible sight was revealed. Lying distortedly in its dishevelled shroud, the staring corpse bore the marks of hideous torment. The hips, knees and forehead were bruised by repeated blows against the interior of the coffin. The fingernails were loosened in the flesh by clawing at the underside of the lid.

If such a frightful end led to the transmission into the living world of information which could have been known only to the departed victim, it must rate as one of the most presageful martyrdoms of all time.

Assailing the infinite with finite resources produces life's most monumental struggle. Dismayed by its magnitude, many turn aside to fill their existence with distractions. Only towards the ending of their span are they reminded that the questions have not gone away. The person who has sought to comprehend the inscrutable may, at the last, be no better blessed with certainty than the individual who has passed his time among the fleshpots. But, given any justice, he should at least find himself in possession of some measure of preparedness for whatever it is that the results of his search suggest awaits him.

We can never hope to know all things. But neither can we expect to silence the curiosity that is part of our nature. Seek, it has been said, and you shall find. My seeking continues.

Bibliography

Chapter

1 Camille Flammarion, *Death and Its Mystery* (Unwin,1922).

5 Harry Price, *The Most Haunted House in England* (Longmans, 1940). Harry Price, *The End of Borley Rectory* (Harrap & Co, 1946). Eric J. Dingwall, Kathleen M. Goldney and Trevor H. Hall, *The Haunting of Borley Rectory* (Duckworth & Co, 1956). Eric J. Dingwall and Trevor H. Hall, *Four Modern Ghosts* (Duckworth & Co, 1958). Robert Hastings, *An Examination of the Borley Report* (The Society for Psychical Research, 1969). Trevor H. Hall, *Search for Harry Price* (Duckworth & Co, 1978). Rev. A.C. Henning, *Haunted Borley*, 1948.

10&14 Ruth Hagy Brod, *Ena Twigg, Medium* (W.H. Allen, 1973).

14 Professor C.E.M. Joad, *The Recovery of Belief* (Faber, 1952). Roger Storey, *Gilbert Harding* (Barrie & Rockliff, 1961).

16 Jan Bryant Bartell, *Spindrift* (New American Library Inc, 1975). Sylvia Barbanell, *When Your Animal Dies* (Spiritualist Press, 1940).

17 Jay Anson, *The Amityville Horror* (W.H. Allen, 1978). H.H. Dukes, *The Physiology of Domestic Animals* (Cornell University Press, 1984).

Index